Have Fun
&
Get It Done

Graduate from a Top University in
3 Years or Less Without Being a Genius!

Jenée Dana

my focus book
Have Fun & Get It Done
Graduate From a Top University
in 3 Years or Less Without Being a Genius

Published by
My Focus Book, LLC
Montebello, California
www.myfocusbook.com

Copyright © 2011 *by Jenée Dana*

Cover Design by Dan Mulhern Design

Interior Design by Dawn Teagarden

Photography by Isis Guzman

ISBN: 978-0-9847-0578-8 (paperback)

Printed in the United States of America

www.myfocusbook.com

Rave Reviews

THE PERFECT BOOK FOR COLLEGE SUCCESS!
Jenee Dana has definitely created an invaluable masterpiece for college students! This piece of art is filled with priceless tools to make sure every student succeeds not only in college, but in all areas of their life. She helps you focus, prioritize, and get it done...fast!

I really wish I had this book while going to college. It took me 5 years to graduate from UCLA and it is only because I didn't know which direction I wanted to go with my life. But if I knew the secrets Jenee has revealed in this book during my time as a student I know would have graduated a lot sooner...without beating myself up.

Her writing style is superb and has a deep understanding for the college student. You can tell it comes from a loving, passionate place. She makes it fun, personable, and stress-free.

Having worked with thousands and thousands of students from around the country and the world I can confidently say that this is a MUST READ for ALL college students, especially for this this generation!

Thank you, Jenee, for what you have put together! This invaluable priceless college success manual will help every student to live the life of their dreams!

> **—Romeo Marquez Jr.** Professor, International Motivational Speaker & Teen Success Coach

How do you say success to the college student of the of the 21st century? "Have Fun and Get it Done". The young people in the 21st century are smart, energetic, knowledgeable and creative. They want to graduate college, travel the world, and be CEO of their own multi-million dollar company all by the age of thirty, and they want to have fun while doing it. In her book," Have Fun and Get it Done", Jenee offers a fool proof philosophy and system on how to successfully complete college while enjoying the experience. It is a witty well-written book that students can relate to and understand. Our future leaders are searching for the secret of how to "Have Fun and Get it Done". Help them out by giving them a book they will read and use to create personal success.

> **—Ahmondra McClendon,** Co-Author of Essence Best Seller Chicken Soup for the African American Soul

www.myfocusbook.com

Taking five upper division courses my last quarter wasn´t easy but I pulled off my last 4.0! It´ll be enough to graduate magna cum laude!

> **—Danny Roddy,** UCLA '12 and featured in the #1 Best Seller 'Have Fun & Get It Done: Graduate From a Top University in 3 Years or Less Without Being a Genius'.

I really like this book. Jenee has a lively style and solid advice.

> **—Dr. Michael J Vendrasco,** Professor at Cal State Fullerton

I highly recommend this book. The author, Jenee Dana is not only witty and clever, but she truly understands the psyche of a pre-college student. I graduated in 3 years from UC Riverside and I can tell you from personal experience that her tips are dead on and will work for anyone that has the passion and drive to succeed. If I had your tips, I think I would have had more fun during the first 2 years.

> **—Victoria Calderon,** UC Riverside '06

We all enjoyed & would recommend this book. Full of good ideas & it speaks to your student in a way that is fun, informative, and can potentially save you, the parent, a ton of moolah. So much of what we deal with at Surf City College Planning is geared towards the financials, the strategies, the FAFSAs, the planning... having folks avoid tapping into their retirement dollars to send their kid(s) to school. HAVE FUN & GET IT DONE fills the missing piece: It speaks directly to the student. Jenee catches your attention at a pivotal point in life, introducing the student early to the importance of DIBS, personal planning, and balance— something we wish we would see more of in the literature. I am adding this to our Student Kits for our College Planning practice. Highly recommend it, and we are ordering a bunch to distribute!

> **—Surf City College Planning,** College Financial Experts

To the Students

For not being afraid to go against the norm...
For not being afraid to ignore those that
discourage you (stupid people)...
And for not being afraid to call DIBS
on your dreams...
This book is for you.

By Jenée Dana

Acknowledgments

This book would not have been written without the support and help of many amazing people in my life.

Adam, the love of my life, the best fiancé in the world, and my rock. I am the luckiest girl on the planet! Thank you for supporting me throughout this entire process, and giving me a push to finish when I needed it most. At the time I didn't look like I appreciated it... hehe...but I did.

I want to thank my mom and grandma (up in heaven), for teaching me how to learn and never give up. I am blessed to have had parents like you. Mom, you have been there for me throughout this entire process. You invested not only in my education but in my business too. You have always believed in me and encouraged me. Without your support, this book would not have happened. I love you.

Deep gratitude goes to the Ramos-Davis, Roman, Chavez, and Castro families who have been like family to me. I love you guys! And I also want to thank the Ron family. I am so grateful for Adam's parents (Mom & Dad), siblings and extended family for welcoming me. I am so blessed to have great family like you. I want to thank the Aceves family for always being there for me, my mom and my grandma when we needed you. I will always be grateful. Uncle Phil, thank you for your support and love.

I want to thank Amanda Johnson. Thank you so much for being an amazing transformational book coach. You are a genius at organizing the structure and flow of a book, and without you, I am not sure this book would have been written. Thank you to everyone in our book mastermind, especially Renee Cabourne and Michele Broad, who were there until the end.

Thank you to Kathy Sparrow for doing an amazing editing job and Lauren Hirchag for proofreading my book. I definitely needed your help and expertise. Special thanks to Isis Guzman for your amazing photography on the cover, Dan Mulhern for your amazing intuitive and creative insights and design of my book cover, and Dawn Teagarden for a beautiful interior layout. You all captured the essence of the book.

To Ursula Mentjes and all of my Quantum Leap Mastermind peeps, thank you for all your valuable feedback. You all inspire me to do greater things and keep going.

Thank you to everyone who let me interview or include them in this book in some way: Professor Tom Gillespie, Professor Michael J. Vendrasco, Katie Ramos, Angie Tam, Larry Broughton, Danny Roddy, Amanda Johnson, Monica Shukla, Derek Sage, Phillip Anthony Lew, Trevor Ramos, and Glenn Morshower. Thank you for your time, as well as your valuable insights and perspectives.

Thank you to Sandra Hanna and *The Smart Cookies* for giving me permission to include your amazing 'Your Perfect Day' Exercise. Every person on this planet needs to do this exercise.

I want to express thanks to all my strategic referral partners and business associates who have supported me along this journey. Special thanks for Ursula Mentjes, Amanda Johnson, Christine Steele, Debra Jarvis, Sean Smith, Lisa Marie Platske, Phil Black, and the entire Productive Learning and Leisure Team.

By Jenée Dana

Thank you original My Focus Book beta testers, Anita Chavez, Analisa Castro, Carol Tuthill, Jamila Robinson, Kimberly Propernick, Danielle Cote, and Alysia Campbell, for helping me to see opportunity when I didn't. You led me to my purpose, which led me to write this book, and I consider you all my great and dear friends. Anita and Analisa...thank you for all the great advice and your friendship.

A special thanks to my principals, teachers, and school counselors at the Montebello Unified School District who believed in me and gave me a basic foundation to build upon. There were some teachers and faculty who really made an extra difference and I want to thank Mrs. Jepsen, Mrs. Brennan, Mrs. Long, Mrs. Montgomery, Mrs. Sanchez-Matos, Mr. Cortez, Mr. Shah ("Nish"), Mr. Wu, Mr. Johnson, Mr.C, Mr.Gomez, Mrs. Cervantes, Mrs. Leboe, Mrs. Sanchez, Mrs. Bayha, Mrs. Barro, Mrs. Monroe, Mr. Schwartz, Mr. Kerr, Mr. Murphy, Ms. Felou, Mr. Angulo, Mrs. Richards, Mr. Smith, and Robert Henke. My deepest gratitude goes to the staff and note takers for the Learning Disabilities Center, the staff and tutors from the Advanced Academic Program (AAP), and the staff and my mentor, Diana, from the Retention of American Indians Now (RAIN) at UCLA. Thank you to Professor M.J. Vendrasco, Professor T.W. Gillespie, Professor L. Smith, and Professor B.L. Barbee at UCLA that taught with passion and helped me stay awake in class. ☺

A big thank you to my friends (you know who you are) who supported me along this crazy-fun journey. Your encouragement and excitement about this book helped keep me going. Thanks for being there for me.

By Jenée Dana

Contents

─────────────────────── PART 2 ───────────────────────

Introduction

If a Pain in the Ass ADHD Social Butterfly Can Get through UCLA in 3 Years, So Can You

"It's kinda fun to do the impossible."

—Walt Disney

My mom and grandma wanted me to start learning early. They had me in preschool at three years old, and they would work with me at home. Both of them noticed that when I didn't understand something right away, I would get upset and frustrated, and throw my pencil or a shoe. Not at them, of course.

When I was getting ready for kindergarten, the ladies in the front office wanted my mom to put me into the advanced class (because my mom was a teacher and they assumed I would be ahead). My mom said, "Oh no. Do you still have the original kindergarten where they socialize (play), sing the alphabet, and count to thirty? Put my daughter in that class. I don't want her to hate school." The ladies were perplexed, but my mom was very smart. She knew exactly what I needed.

I loved school. Being an only child, I loved being around tiny people like me all day. And since I was in the easy class, frustrations were minimal during the transition. But when I got to first grade, I felt stupid and slow compared to the other kids. It took me longer to learn how to read, and I *knew* I was getting extra help at home, which just added to the frustration.

At my school, our grading system was a little different. We had Os for Outstanding, which was the equivalent of an "A". Ss were Satisfactory, which was a C. ✓s were like Ds or Fs. My friend Katie would ALWAYS get straight Os and get pissed whenever she got one S.

Looking back at my report cards, there were twenty different categories of skills and knowledge. I would get straight Ss, and the only Os I got were in "Socializing". I am NOT making that up. I would always wonder why I couldn't be smart like Katie, and I wasn't the only one questioning my abilities. At the end of my second grade parent-teacher conference, my teacher told my mom she thought I was going to grow up and be a great cheerleader.

Okay, you will hear me say often that you can be whatever you want to be. There is absolutely nothing wrong with cheerleaders. I think it would be awesome to be a professional NFL cheerleader. However, there was a certain connotation and stereotype of cheerleaders that came along with this remark that my mom didn't appreciate. Of course, I had no clue what she meant at the time and was excited about throwing around the pom poms.

By Jenée Dana

But I kept working hard in school, and by middle school, I was on the honor roll, getting mostly As with a couple Bs here and there. By high school, I had a 4.2 GPA. Four years later, I was accepted to UCLA. Woohooo! I had made it! But during my freshman year at the big university, I had another wake-up call. I suddenly felt stupid again when stacked up against the competition.

One day in my dorm, a couple of floor mates stopped by and jumped into a conversation I was having with my roommate. For some reason, one of the boys asked her, "So what was your SAT score?" My roommate seemed to blush and said, "Oh gosh, it is so awful and low. I don't want to say." He prodded and she finally gave in and said, "1420." The two boys had scores of 1520 and 1560. Then they all turned to me. "What was your score?" I was sweating. "1140," I blurted out. And do you know what my asinine floor mate with all of his jackassery said? "What are YOU doing here?" As if I didn't deserve to be a student at UCLA!?!

All the feelings from elementary school of not being smart enough came rushing back and made my stomach turn. I was really hurt by what he said, and I wanted to say, *"Well, while you were at SAT camp being a nerd, I was playing water polo, having fun with my friends and still managing to get good grades."* Unfortunately, I said that in my head and not to that troll.

What trolls (like my hall-mate) should you stay away from?

But the truth was that my freshman year of college in my first quarter of school, I got the LOWEST midterm grade of about 180 students. It was the ugliest F you can get. When my professor posted a chart of the average grades of the midterm, my grade was all the way to the left of the chart all by itself, which meant it was really bad!

However, after I learned how to study for college tests and value my time, I never saw a grade like that again. In fact, I got a 3.4 GPA in my major, Geography and Environmental Studies, and 3.3 overall. My senior year, with a double load of classes and working, I got a 3.5 GPA. The other students I interviewed for this book got some great grades too. Katie got a 3.9, Danny currently has a 3.8 and I don't know Angie's GPA, but it was up there.

I am not afraid to admit when people might be more

By Jenée Dana

talented than me in certain areas. In fact, I started getting even better grades my senior year while taking a double load because I wasn't afraid to admit someone was better than me at something, or learn from them. I studied with Angie, and she gave me amazing study tips. What I discovered my senior year was that most of the time, it's not that people are actually smarter; they just have better ways of doing things or they have a strength that complements your weakness.

Who do you know that gets really good grades (but isn't an annoying, self-proclaimed genius)? Learn to study with them.

When I tell people I graduated UCLA in 3 years, they have all kinds of questions for me: *How did you do that? Why would you do that? Didn't you want to have fun while you were in college? Do you think I could do that?*

My response to that last question is always, "If this pain in the ass ADHD social butterfly can get through UCLA in 3 years, so can you." And the rest of those questions are the reason I decided to write this book. There are too many people – especially young people – in the world who simply don't know what they are capable of doing because they don't even know it is an option to do more. Or no one has taught them the skills and tools they need to succeed *and* have a blast doing it.

I had SO MUCH FUN my last year of college. By the time I completed my second year, I had figured out how to value my time, study effectively, and have as much fun as I wanted to have. I had figured out how to *Have Fun & Get It Done.*

Remember that second grade teacher? "She'll be a great cheerleader someday." Well, she did get something right: Today I have a successful and growing business that teaches students how to graduate early, *and* sales professionals and entrepreneurs how to increase their productivity and their income, all while having a life that (by their definition) is *awwwwwessssome.* I *cheer* them on as they accomplish all their goals and check off experiences on their bucket lists.

Who woulda thunk it was possible for a gurl like me? LOL! ☺

I'm not telling you any of this to brag about how great I am. I just want to inspire the possibilities in you. If I can do it – you can do it!

But how? I know that's the question you're asking, and that's why I've written this book. People asked me HOW?

But before we talk about HOW, there are other questions that should be asked and answered first:

- *What does the 4-year plan look like?*
- *What does a 3-year plan normally look like?*
- *What do you really want?*
- *Which plan makes the most sense for you?*

Once you get the answers to these questions in Part 1, you'll be READY for the goal-setting and achievement, life management, studying, and social survival tools and strategies provided in Part 2.

Also ask yourself: *Is college even right for me?* Did I mention that you do not have to go to college to be successful? Before your parents hate me, college is not the only place to receive intellectual development. It is just a popular place to do so. There are many trade schools that can provide the skills you need to make a good living. There are certificate programs, all types of seminars, and – gosh darnit – you can even pick up a book or read an article online from a reliable source. Bill Gates dropped out of college and would you say that he is not smart or a highly intellectual person? No. I know, I am writing a book on how to graduate in 3 years and telling you that college may not be the answer. Sounds crazy, right? But I want you to ask these questions for yourself. This is not about me – it is about you.

Oh, and I think I said this already, but in my college experience, I learned so much from asking other students how they were doing so well in class that I've decided to include stories and tips from other successful students, entrepreneurs, and even a well-known actor.

I want you to be able to learn from all of our experiences, take what is most useful for you, and jump into action.

Let's have fun and get it done together!

By Jenée Dana

Part 1

Rockin' Your Undies

Learning Your Options, Figuring Out the Best Path
for You, & Rockin' It

"Don't be afraid to fail. The greatest failure
of all is failure to act when action is needed.
Use the information that you've acquired in
the past through the experiences you've had
and act with self-control — but act."

John Wooden

The first four chapters of this book are designed to introduce you to the benefits of the 4-year plan and the 3-year plan, help you figure out what you want, and then show you how to create your plan to get it. If you don't know what your options are, then it's hard to make a good decision.

There will be self-reflection questions along the way to help you figure out what is best for you. I suggest you fill them out as you read the chapter, so you won't forget to do it later. (It's great practice for taking notes in college!)

By Jenée Dana

Chapter 1

The Benefits of Granny Panties & Tighty Whities

The Traditional Route Can Feel Comfortable and Safe

"Don't let the noise of other's opinions drown out your own inner voice. And most important, have the courage to follow your heart and intuition. They somehow already know what you truly want to become. Everything else is secondary."

Steve Jobs

Have you ever worn granny panties or tighty whities? They are comfortable; no wedgies, no pressure. That is what the traditional graduation route is like for many students, and there are many benefits to graduating in 4 or more years. It is important to know what these benefits are, so you can weigh them against the benefits of the 3-year plan. It is also a good idea to take a look at how much college costs today, especially as the average time it takes to get a degree is increasing. Is spending an extra $20,000, $50,000, or more going to affect your future?

Traditional Time-Frame

Traditional routes have always followed a 4-year plan. Generally speaking, the first two years are meant to expose young people to all of their options, and the last two years are focused on preparing them for their chosen career path.

Traditional Cost

After talking with Phillip Lew, America's Leading Authority on College Planning, I discovered that when you understand how much college truly costs, it can help you decide which college is best for you. You can also make a logical financial decision regarding whether you want to graduate using a 3-year or 4-year plan by maximizing the amount of financial aid you can receive.

When people look at going to college, they usually only pay attention to the big numbers of tuition and room and board, but it's important to take a look at the true cost with all of those little things that add up to a lot.

- Tuition and fees
- Room and board
- Travel / Transportation
- Books and other supplies
- Personal expenses (realistically, these expenses are about five to seven times larger than what a college will estimate for you on their website)

Your Cost of Attendance will vary depending on THREE factors:

1. Whether you are a resident or non-resident (out of state) student

2. Whether you attend public or private school, and

3. Whether you will live at home, in an apartment, or on campus

The graphs below are averages of what college will cost in 2011 in California depending on where you decide to live. These are only averages and can vary from different schools and states.

Living On-campus

	California Community College	California State Universities (CSU)	University of California (UC)	California Private Universities
Fees	$780	$5,198	$11,603	$43,306
Books & Supplies	$1,566	$1,624	$1,543	$1,500
Room & Board	$7,800**	$10,368	$12,780	$12,078
Transportation	$1,060	$1,060	$1,055	$2,000
Personal	$2,394	$2,619	$1,746	$2,934
Total	$13,600	$20,869	$27,184	$61,818

Living Off-campus

	California Community College	California State Universities (CSU)	University of California (UC)	California Private Universities
Fees	$780	$5,198	$11,603	$43,306
Books & Supplies	$1,566	$1,624	$1,543	$1,500
Room & Board	$11,153	$11,153	$9,302	$10,506
Transportation	$1,188	$1,188	$1,686	$1,617
Personal	$3,546	$2,656	$2,290	$3,024
Total	$17,233	$21,819	$26,424	$59,953

By Jenée Dana

Living with Parents

	California Community College	California State Universities (CSU)	University of California (UC)	California Private Universities
Fees	$780	$5,198	$11,603	$43,306
Books & Supplies	$1,566	$1,624	$1,543	$1,500
Room & Board	$4,266	$4,257	$4,360	$4,387
Transportation	$1,196	$1,196	$1,895	$2,003
Personal	$3,528	$2,706	$2,389	$3,112
Total	$11,336	$14,981	$21,790	$54,308

**Remember, your personal expenses will likely be five to seven times more than what the universities averages suggest.

You can get more specific estimates by looking at college brochures and websites. Or you can go to http://collegesearch.collegeboard.com/ search/adv_typeofschool.jsp in order to compare costs at more than 3,800 universities.

Traditional Funding

So, now that you can see how much this college thing is going to cost you every year, it's time to talk about how you're going to pay for it. At Phillip Lew's workshop, I learned that parents and students have multiple ways of paying for college:

1. Loans

2. Federal Loans

3. Private Bank Loans

4. Parents' Moola / Savings

5. Extra Job: Work while you go to school

6. Financial Aid and Grants

   Financial aid and grants are provided to students in three different categories: Need-based, Merit-based, and Endowment-based.

   • Need-based

      $$COA - EFC = NEED$$
      (cost of attendance – expected family contribution = need)

      • Gift Aid (grants and scholarships)

      • Self-help Aid (student loans and federal work study)

   • Merit-based

      Academic or Athletic scholarships

      • These scholarships are earned based on your academic or athletic ranking among your peers. Those students in the top percentiles of their college have better chances of receiving these scholarships.

By Jenée Dana

- Endowment-based

    Any reason the college wants

    - Being a "diversity" student can sometimes qualify you for financial aid. For example, if you are a female student applying to major in Quantum Physics, you would be considered a "diversity" student if that major was overrun with male students and they wanted to attract more female students.

7. Private Scholarships

    - If you've excelled in academics or sports, you may be offered a private scholarship. However, private scholarships account for only 5% of the total amount of scholarship and grant money available.

8. Combination of any of the above

Why Pay Retail for College?

Phillip Lew is an expert at teaching students and parents how to cut down the sticker price of college. In his book *Phillip Lew's College Planning System for Success*, he breaks down how a private college can actually cost less than a public college in one of his case studies.

School A:	School B:
PRIVATE College	PUBLIC College
Cost - $40,000	Cost - $20,000
EFC- $10,000	EFC - $10,000
Need - $30,000	Need - $10,000
School A: Meet Need?	**School B: Meet Need?**
Meets 100% need	Meets 60% need = $6,000
Gift aid – 80%	($4,000 in unmet need!)
Self help – 20%	Gift aid – 50%
	Self help – 50%
School A: Breakdown	**School B: Breakdown**
Total EFC = $10,000	EFC = $10,000
Total Gift = $24,000	+Unmet Need = $4,000
Total Self = $6,000	Total EFC = $14,000
	Total Gift = $3,000
	Total Self = $3,000
School A:	**School B:**
Total Out of Pocket Cost	**Total Out of Pocket Cost**
$16,000 per year	$17,000 per year
($10,000 EFC + $6,000 self help)	(10,000 EFC + $7,000 self help)

The private school met 100% of the need, but the public school only provided for 60% of the need. Instead of the private school costing $160,000 for 4 years (their sticker price), it would only cost $64,000. The public school ends up costing $4,000 more for a 4-year degree at $17,000 per year.

By Jenée Dana

There is a lot more information on how to get financial aid, even if you don't think you qualify, and how to get the best wholesale price for college. You can read Phillip's book or go to his website at www.totalcollegesolutions.com for more information.

Traditional Track in Recessions

During a recession, the traditional 4-year plan turns into something more like a 5-7 year plan because budgets are cut in state schools and fewer classes are offered, making it a little bit harder for students to get the classes they want. When looking at schools, ask how long it takes their students to graduate on average.

If it takes someone between four and seven years to graduate, with the average cost of yearly tuition and fees at a public 4-year college, it could cost anywhere from $70,000-$119,000 out of pocket. That's an additional $49,000. Remember I said out of pocket: I am not counting gift aid. Not to mention the cost of opportunity. By taking one to three extra years to graduate, you are not just paying extra for school. You are also, most likely, not bringing in a full-time income. Let's say your starting salary would be $50,000. With an extra three years in school, you are racking up extra debt *and* losing $150,000 in potential income.

Traditional Choices

You might have a bunch of different reasons for choosing your school. If you are really clear about where you are headed, you may choose a school that has a good reputation in that chosen career field. If you have no idea what to do, you may choose a junior college or university with an overall great reputation.

Below you will find some of the motivating factors or values that drive people to choose one type of school over the other, and you'll see what my process looked like as well.

- **Reputation and Career Path**

   I didn't know what my major was going to be. Since I was undecided, I couldn't pick a school that was the best for a particular major, so I picked UCLA because it had the best overall reputation. Think about it. When people say they went to 'Harvard' or 'West Point', do you really care what they majored in? No. Just hearing the name Harvard is enough because of the reputation attached to it.

- **Location**

   UCLA was far enough away from home to move out and be on my own, but close enough to still see my mom and friends in case I got homesick. Yes, I chickened out on moving far away or out of state, but at the time it wasn't my priority.

- **Money**

   When my mom went to school, she didn't qualify for financial aid because her family's income was $200 over the yearly limit. She had to work full-time in order to support herself while going to school. My grandparents just could not afford to pay for her studies while raising five other kids. While she didn't want me to stress about how to pay for school, I could see the worry in her face sometimes, which is one of the reasons I wanted to graduate early.

Why Would You Stay 4 Years?

There are benefits to a 4-year plan that are really determined by your values and preferences.

If You Love College

Some people just love college. Some enjoy the learning – they love books. For others, college is a big PARTY!

If you are a person who tends to love learning, then you may really enjoy all four years. For me, I love to learn BUT learning was difficult my first two years. Midterms and finals are not my thing. Four years sounded like torture to me by the end of my second year, but I do have friends who really enjoyed their college years and would have stayed longer. In fact, by applying my life management and study tips early on in your college career, you could actually become one of those people who really like to learn and have fun.

An extra year of clubs, sports games, parties, etc. make the extra year super appealing to some people. I get that. If you really, really love college activities and never want to leave, then perhaps being an event planner would be an ideal career for you. If you love the learning aspect of college and research, maybe a professor position would be ideal for you.

One of my professors at UCLA loved his job. He loved the fact that he could come to school at 11am for a lecture and the rest of the day was his to design as long as he got his research done for his journals. He was passionate about his work, his research, and he loved his life.

My first year in the dorms, we had a mini prank war. My friend and floor mate Angie had this ugly looking monster creature that sticks inside of a toilet bowl. She kept asking me if I had to go to the bathroom while I was writing a paper. I thought it was strange, but I was so preoccupied, I wasn't paying attention. Finally, she gave up and left my room to go to bed. My roommate Nicole fell asleep as I stayed up late crunching out my last-minute paper. At one o'clock in the morning, I finally had to pee. My glasses were off and without them I am almost as blind as a bat. I can see, but it is all blurry. I lifted up the toilet seat and these arms flailed upward and there was some sort of ugly blurry red thing in the toilet. I freaked out, jumped backwards, almost falling into my closet. The PRANK WAR was on! Since Nicole knew this ugly contraption was in the toilet, I ripped it out from the pearly bowl and placed it ever so gently in front of her peaceful sleeping face. I woke up to her screaming. It was GLORIOUS!

By Jenée Dana

36

If You Want to See the World

You may want more time to study abroad if that is something on your bucket list. Danny, who we will talk about later in this book, could have also graduated UCLA in 3 years but decided that he wanted to take a year to explore the world and get school credit for it. I think that was a really smart decision. It made sense for him, and it's what he wanted.

If You Want to Be Involved

You may be really involved in some clubs or sports organizations at your school and may just want another year to enjoy your involvement with them. Some of you have friends that you entered with as a freshman, and you want to graduate with them as a senior. Makes sense.

Now it was finals week, and my brain was fried. So Nicole and I decided to get the original prankster Angie back. We each took a four-foot stack of the Daily Bruin newspaper and brought it back to our room. We crumbled up paper until 4am (while eating pizza) and then covered the gap between the hallway and Angie's door with newspaper, filling the gap up to the top with balls of the paper and other random items. (Note: The paper was a day old and was going to be thrown out. Technically, we weren't wasting it.) So when she opened her door to leave for her final in the morning, Angie was greeted with a newspaper shower. Lame prank...I know. (I was an oober goober...brains were fried.)

For revenge, Angie snatched my stuffed monkey, took a picture of him being "held up" by a banana, and emailed it to me with a ransom note: "Deliver $50,000 pesos or the monkey gets it!"

By Jenée Dana

If You Like Your Breaks

The 4-year plan means you probably don't have to take any summer school. However, for the schools that think you need to go to school Monday through Friday for a foreign language, I highly suggest that you take that class in summer school and don't make the same mistake I did. In college you get used to only having classes two to three days a week. One day I was not paying attention when signing up for my year-long foreign language requirement. I thought it was Monday, Wednesday, Friday, but it turns out it was Monday through Friday and they dinged your grade if you didn't show up. That was a load of crap and a lot of gas money as I commuted from home that year.

If You Want More than One Major

Depending on the majors and how your requirements overlap, you can double or maybe even triple major. If that's important to you and your career goals, then you may need to stick to the 4-year plan although Monica, who shares tips later in this book, graduated in 3 years with two degrees.

If You're Not Sure What You Want to Do

Ideally, it is awesome to explore your possibilities if you're not 100% sure what you want to do for a career when you get to college. While you are exploring, you discover things you like, things you love, and things you hate, which means that you will spend some additional time checking out your options and figuring it all out. Some people don't figure it out until they're in the third year, and then they have two years of studying that major ahead of them.

There is this ugly myth that you are never going to have as much fun in life as you did in college. I have to disagree. This might be true if you just take a job for money and hate what you do, but life continues to be fun and adventurous for those who continue to do what they love. College is a different experience in life, and if you want to continue that experience for four years or more, there is nothing wrong with that, as long as you are educated in how much it costs.

Whether you prefer granny panties and tighty whities for the comfort, or you want to explore new options like the bikini or boxer brief (oh so sexy), it's good to know all of your options before you decide.

Chapter 2

Be an Underwear Rebel: Enter the World of Bikinis & Boxer Briefs

Discover the Benefits of the New 3-year Plan

"Never be afraid to try something new.
Remember, amateurs built the ark;
professionals built the Titanic."

Author Unknown

No offense to granny panties and tighty whities, but bikinis and boxer briefs are sexy and fun, while still providing a certain level of comfort. Hmmm...sexy and comfortable. I like that. Okay, so the 3-year plan isn't literally sexy, but the fact that not many students explore this route, and that it is faster yet totally doable, makes it an attractive option.

When I share about my experience of graduating UCLA in three years, I'm always surprised to hear people say things like, "I didn't even know that someone could graduate in three years. I didn't think it was really possible without killing yourself," "How is that possible?", and "Why would someone want to put themselves through that anyway?"

I didn't know it was possible either until I was really feeling the need to "get out of Dodge". Over time, I've met lots of people who I knew would really have been so much happier had they known about the possibility earlier and taken full advantage of it. So, here it is – the possibility spelled out in SIMPLE terms!

Why graduate in 3 years?

You Might Not Like School

Let's face it, college isn't for everyone. Some people really don't like school and never have – either because of negative experiences or just because they're bored and have the feeling there are better ways for them to spend their time. (Me! Me! Me!) The first two years of college I had some fun, but I was more stressed out than anything else. I couldn't understand why I couldn't pay attention in class, midterms freaked me out, and I couldn't enjoy the present moment when all my work and tests were hanging over my head. I was so relieved when I found out I had ADHD and wasn't stupid.

On a scale of 1 – 10, how much do you like school? (1 = school is asinine, 10 = school is awesome) What would school need to be like in order to make it a 10 for you?

By Jenée Dana

If you have not enjoyed school that much because you have felt like you don't learn as fast as everyone else and it seems daunting, I have two recommendations for you:

1. Check out the life management tools and study strategies in Chapters 6 and 7, and then TRY THEM. Really give them your best shot.

2. If these tools don't seem to help, ask your parents or high school counselor for support. Tell them exactly how you feel in class or when you try to study. It may be that you have a learning obstacle (like I did!) and they could help you find a way to diagnose it and provide solutions. Obstacle courses are meant to be conquered, so having a learning obstacle is not a setback – it's a learning curve.

One major item to check if you really hate school is your major. Have you picked a major yet?

Sometimes all the options and the feeling of not knowing your direction can be overwhelming.

Are you enjoying what you are learning? If you are picking a major just for the thought of having a good job after graduating, but you aren't enjoying what you are learning, you might want to go back to the drawing board and really listen to yourself. What do you love to do? What fascinates you? Otherwise, you're wasting your time and money in school only to end up in a job you will probably hate, just for the money. Don't worry. It doesn't have to be that way.

I am hoping that after reading this book and applying the life management skills you learn in the in the upcoming chapters, your entire college experience will be full of fun and stress will be a fleeting thought (like a loser ex after you start dating someone even better).

You Might Want to Start a Business

While you can most definitely run a business while you are in school, if your business is more fun than school itself, you might be tempted to pay more attention to your business than your studies.

I know a business owner, Derek Sage, who started his business when he was 11 years old. By the time he was in high school, he had a very successful DJ and event production company (www.SOSentertainment.com). When he got into college, his company was doing about 45 events a year and was ready to expand. He noticed that he was paying less attention to schoolwork and was completely devoted to his business. When he began failing his college classes after previously getting As, he realized that he was already doing what he loved to do and making good money at it. He decided to leave school and expand his business. Just because Derek left school does not mean he stopped learning. Among other things, he studied Chinese on his own, and over the course of four years, he became fluid in the language. There are plenty of very successful people who never made it all the way through college. Mark Zuckerberg, the founder and owner of Facebook, quit Harvard when he started his business. I don't think his parents are very disappointed in their son.

IMPORTANT NOTE: I am *NOT* telling you to quit school. If you own a business, or want to start a business, you might find a way to mesh the two together. Maybe you can incorporate your business work into the papers you have to write and the projects you have to complete. Double-dipping is highly recommended.

While you may want to make your parents proud, you also need to be happy. It is your life. I figured if I graduated a year early, I could focus my full attention on whatever I wanted after that. I didn't know what I wanted at the time, and I was busy trying to figure it out. In the process, I ended up learning how to have fun and still get everything done, and my passion and purpose started to unfold.

You're Planning to Go to Grad School

Grad school is expensive, and less financial aid is available for grad school than for undergrad degrees. Why not cut down your student loan totals by a year's tuition so you can apply that money to grad school? Also, some grad schools, like MBA programs, prefer that you have work experience before you join the program, and graduating a year early will allow you to get a head start on your work experience and your graduate studies.

You Want More than One Degree

If you can get at least one degree in 3 years, you could get two degrees in 4 years if you decide you're having a lot of fun and would like to stay an extra year. Monica earned four degrees in 5 years from Chapman University.

You Want Avoid a Year of Midterms and Finals

Part of me loved college, but my first two years I can honestly say I hated tests, research papers, midterms, and finals. I love to learn, but the pressure of getting good grades at a top university was freaking me out and giving me hives. I literally broke out with eczema all over my body. It was embarrassing and I didn't want anyone to see me. I was so stressed out because I didn't have the right tools – the time management tools and study skills – to allow me to get more done and CHILL-AX. Luckily, I figured out how to study more effectively and value my time. In fact, I almost didn't want to leave after my third year because it was so amazingly fun.

By Jenée Dana

46

It Looks Great on Job Applications

Unless the hiring manager is a complete idiot and allergic to common sense, graduating from any top university in 3 years or less is impressive. It shows that not only are you smart enough to figure out how to be successful in your position, you work fast and effectively. Most companies are concerned with their bottom line. The more productive you are, the less money you cost them. Plain and simple.

You Can Save a Year's Worth of Tuition and Expenses (approx. $12,000-$80,000)

Each year adds on a year of tuition, books, and room and board. Now if you've got a lot of scholarships or financial aid, then this isn't as much of a big deal. But it is if you don't have the luxury of an all (or most) expenses paid education. One of the main motivators for me to graduate early was to save my mom a year of tuition in school.

Even though my mom was a single parent and I qualified for Cal grants for Cal State Universities, I didn't qualify for any financial aid from UCLA. Can you tell I am still a little peeved about that? I felt a little guilty for dropping a full ride at another university to go to the "better name" school and costing my mom all that money. To help her out, I wanted to graduate early to save her at least a year's worth of college expenses since I could have saved her four years with my free ride. I know that she was happy to write that check to UCLA because she was going to get that piece of paper confirming my BA degree at the end of it. It made me feel better knowing I was helping her out.

You might be in a similar situation where you are just on the cusp of not qualifying for financial aid. I can feel your pain and worry. I suggest you check out Philip Lew's website (www.totalcollegesolutions.com). If you combine graduating early with getting more financial aid, you could save a lot of money and possibly lighten the student loan burden.

Knowing what I know now, I never recommend making life and career decisions *solely* based on money. I know that sounds weird and, for some people, absolutely ridiculous. It is best to base all of your decisions on what you want and what is going to make you happy. The money will follow. If you are truly passionate about something, there is usually a way to figure out how to make any situation a win-win.

Not all colleges offer block tuition—a flat tuition fee—no matter how many units you take. However, most private schools and popular state schools like UCLA do. More colleges and universities are converting to this method. Check to see if it is offered at your school and take advantage of it.

By Jenée Dana

There's More to Life than School.
Life is School.

Maybe there's something that you want to do before you settle down and have kids that isn't school related. Graduating a year early can give you an excuse to do those things before you get started on the rest your "adult" life. I'm not talking about anything illegal here. I'm just saying maybe you want to backpack through Europe for a year without having to think about class. Maybe you want to build schools in Africa. Or maybe you just want to vegetate and meditate. Using a 3-year plan approach to your education gives you a little wiggle room in your post-graduation planning.

By now, you should have an idea what you would gain by choosing the traditional 4-year plan or changing it up for the 3-year option. Whether you prefer old school panties or a hot college experience is up to you. It doesn't matter what everyone else thinks. What matters is what you value the most. The next chapter will help you do some self-reflection so you can figure out what you really want to achieve in your life and in your college experiences.

Notes:

If you had one
year to do whatever you
wanted, what would you do?

What do you need, or who
do you need to ask, to make
sure you get what
you want?

Chapter 3

Finding Your Undie Style

Deciding What's Right For You:
What Do YOU Want?

"You don't want to get to the top of the
ladder only to find out you had it leaning up
against the wrong wall."

Jack Canfield

Right now you might be feeling an immense amount of pressure if you don't know exactly what you want to do in life. You may have never even asked yourself the question, "What is my purpose?" Or maybe you know exactly what you love to do, but you are afraid it is not going to please your parents, or provide a comfortable financial lifestyle for you. Or maybe you thought you knew exactly what you wanted, and after trying it, you realize you don't like it and are back to "square one."

I have experienced every one of these feelings, and so has everyone else. In case you were worried, don't be! You're normal! Just like we match our clothes style, and even our undies style, to our personality, we want to figure out our *life*-style and have that match with who we are and what we value most.

Pressures in life and in school can distract you from asking yourself important questions and thinking about what you really want in life. Sometimes we get so caught up in trying to please or impress everyone else, we forget to stop and impress ourselves.

What pressure cooker are you in?
(circle all that apply)

- Stressing out about earning good grades so you can get accepted into college or grad school?
- Balancing school, homework, and all of your activities?
- Dating train wrecks?
- Trying to impress your parents?
- Breaking out all over your face?
- Feeling lost because you don't know what you want and feel unmotivated?
- Having to pick a major?
- Fearing that you'll mess up or make a mistake?
- Wondering why your parents gave you this book and how they can expect you to have this all figured out already?

Sometimes all these things can weigh on you and take away from your awesome-sauce. Chill out! It's okay. Just try the exercises in this chapter and always use your heart in conjunction with your mind. When you use them separately, you either chase a white rabbit down a rabbit hole or do the robot-icized logical thing. Either way, you could easily end up being completely miserable.

Are you passionate? Or did you pass-on-it?

When I was in high school, I had to wake up for zero period because I was in the band and then I had either band, water polo, or swimming practice after school. I would usually get home between 6pm and 9pm, depending on what activity I had, and then I would have to shower (rinse off all the chlorine), eat dinner (usually three plates full because I was in sports), and then do my homework until 1 or 2am.

I was so busy trying to be a "well-rounded" student, I was just doing things to "do" them and not really taking the time to think about what I wanted to do for the rest of my life. Don't get me wrong, I liked water polo and swimming, and I was having a great time. BUT I wasn't passionate about water polo, and that was the difference. I didn't learn this 'til after college. Just because you like something doesn't mean you are passionate about it and can do it for the next 40 years of your life.

The same thing happened in college. I was so stressed out about midterms and finals that I was not focusing on the main reason why I was there: *To find and expand on my passions.*

There is no one right path, but determining the path that is right for you is the most important. Life is too short to be doing a bunch of CRAP you hate. ***Lean into what you love.*** Follow your interests and be open to opportunities that come along the way. When you follow your interests, you can find your passion. Your passion could unfold into a dream career you never expected. When you get to act on what you love every day, you never *really* "work" another day in your life.

"Lose yourself in your passion and find yourself in your journey."

By Jenée Dana

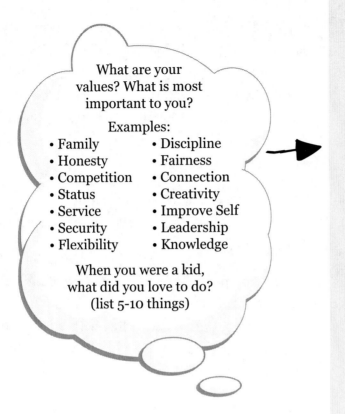

Think about this: The jobs of 2020 haven't even been created yet. One hundred years ago we didn't have cell phones. I got my first cell phone ten years ago, when they were becoming mainstream. Now cell phones have provided thousands of job and business opportunities. Three years ago, I would have said, "What the hell is an APP?" And now that APPs are gaining popularity, they are creating many job and business opportunities as well. Now I am creating a web application so students and entrepreneurs can have fun and get it all done. It's called *My Focus Book App* (www.myfocusbook.com). There are even Social Media Managers and Consultants now. How many of you are on Twitter or Facebook all day? 99.99% of the time, there is a way to turn your passions into a very comfortable living.

Once you are crystal clear on what makes you happy and brings you the most joy, you can more easily determine your purpose.

In fact, your passions and interests are often clues to your purpose – the reason why you are on the planet. And when your goals are in line with your purpose, you will experience more joy and happiness. It's one big luscious circle.

When you are clear on what your purpose is and what you want, you achieve your goals much faster because you are aware of the opportunities that come to you.

Did you know you have a Reticular Activating System (RAS) that is your brain's filter for the 8 million bits of information that constantly stream through it? As the filter, the RAS only lets in important information for survival and getting what we want. This is how it works:

> Have you ever been shopping for a car and all of a sudden you see the car you want, or model, or color everywhere? And then you think, 'Gosh!

Everyone is thinking like me and went out and bought this car all at the same time!!!'

No. Those cars were there on the road before you went shopping. You just noticed them because that is the "want" that you were *focused* on at the moment. Amazing, huh?

Passion is that spark inside of you – it's what gives you butterflies and lights your eyes up.

Monica Shukla figured out what her passion was in chemistry lab.

I thought I was going to the University of California Irvine after getting into their Engineering program. I wanted to stay close to home. My counselor said it would take six years to graduate with a BA in Engineering. My Dad was teaching at Chapman University, and I found out that Chapman has a joint program with UCI. I could get a Math or Chemistry degree at Chapman in three years, then transfer to UCI and get the Engineering degree in two years. I thought this was great. I would get two degrees and shave off a year of school.

My father had a background in Business and my mom a background in Science, so I thought getting a degree in Chemistry and Engineering would be a clear 1 – 2 – 3 path.

1. bachelor's degree
2. master's degree
3. great job

By Jenée Dana

A year and a half into the program at Chapman, I was taking Organic Chemistry, Quantitative Analysis, Physics 2 and Multi-variable Calculus with a Meditation class for sanity.
And I was spending:

- 12-15 hours per week in lab
- at least 30 hours per week studying

It didn't take long for me to realize math was coming naturally to me, and I enjoyed it. I was completely calm if a pop quiz came up in math while I had to force myself to like chemistry, and it wasn't working too well.

My Dad said, "Do something you can do the next forty years of your life."

I found myself sitting in my chemistry lab on Friday afternoon watching the chemicals reflux (boil), while my friends were at the beach, and I realized I couldn't do this for another four minutes!

I jumped up and immediately started packing up my lab. When my professor asked me if I was okay, I told him, "I'm alright. I will send you an email." I went straight to the Registrar Office and switched my major to Math instantly. It was the best decision of my life.

Because the Math program was so much more fun and easy for me, I started taking other classes outside my major (Communications and Public Speaking) that I enjoyed. I ended up taking so many that by the time I was ready to graduate, I only needed three more classes for a Communications degree. So, in three years and one semester, I had acquired two degrees.

By Jenée Dana

I started my master's in Human Resources to utilize both majors and the same thing happened. When I was graduating in January of 2008, I only needed five or six more classes for a second masters in Leadership. So, I graduated in August of 2008 with two bachelor's degrees and two masters' in five years.

Now I work full time at Chapman University as a Career Employer Outreach Manager. I also own and run a successful college planning and tutoring company (www.advancetocollege.com), and I am studying for my Ph.D. in Cultural and Curriculum Studies.

My advice: It's not about getting the job that pays the most money. I was going to major in Engineering because of the high paying starting salaries, but I learned that life is about doing what you love, what makes you happy, and what provides the lifestyle you want.

Monica Shukla

Danny Roddy is currently attending UCLA. And although he could have graduated in 3 years, he decided to study abroad for a year.

I am a history major and absolutely love it! I have loved history ever since my Uncle Rich taught me about Julius Caesar and Cleopatra. I was six years old.

I went in "undeclared" because I was scared of picking a major that would limit my options after I got my undergraduate degree. But by sophomore year, I decided to go with what I love. I realized every degree has its value. Your best bet is to major in something you love and are good at. When I worked at the UCLA Call Center, I even talked to a UCLA grad who had been a history major, completed his LS series, and ended up going to medical school. After I graduate, I plan to become a history professor, which has been my dream job since freshman year in high school. Whether rambling on to my friends or helping tutor kids who need help in history classes, I have always loved to teach, talk about, and write about history.

By Jenée Dana

I realized that graduating in 3 years wasn't the best choice for me. I was having a lot of fun at UCLA and wanted to make sure I got everything I could out of my time there. Even taking it to my senior year, I am still going to graduate at 21 years old.

Going to Europe was a way for me to not only extend my time at UCLA, but also to travel (which was one of my long time aspirations). I used to think there was this huge rush to graduate and start my life, but, after talking to family and friends, I realized that I am at one of the best universities in the country, I am only going to be in college for a short period of my life, and I am young. Why not enjoy it while I can?

Danny Roddy

Perfect Day Exercise

Imagine yourself 2-7 years from now and work through this exercise from the Smart Cookies.

www.smartcookies.com

Imagine it is Wednesday morning.

Think about exactly how you want to spend that day. Keep in mind that it's a weekday, so you still have work, but consider the type of work you do during that perfect day. Finally, use the questions below to develop a description of your Perfect Day.

- What time do you wake up, and how are you feeling as you face the day?
- Where are you?
- If you're at home, what does that look like?
- Who is with you?
- People?
- Pets?
- What are your activities that day?

By Jenée Dana

- What kind of work do you undertake and with whom? Consider the qualities you want in the work you do, including the ideal workplace environment.
- As you head to work, what are you wearing and how do you look?
- When and where do you work, and how do you get there? (Super important to think about if you hate traffic. Stress caused from traffic takes years off your life.)
- When work is done, what do you do with your spare time?
- Who do you spend your time with and how do you relax?
- What is your evening like?
- What do you eat for dinner?
- Who are you with?
- As your day winds down, what are you grateful for?
- What are you excited about as you drift off to sleep?
- What are you looking forward to?

I didn't find my purpose instantaneously. It was through a series of events that I realized what I wanted to do for the rest of my life.

I always knew that I was stubborn about having fun and my quality time with friends or family. Sometimes my mom just didn't understand that I needed my fun time in order to recharge. In her mind, the dishes had to be done and the car had to be washed. Life, to me, isn't about work, work, work. Yes, "things" need to get done. But if you don't make time for the good life, what's the point of all the other stuff you have to do?

After I graduated UCLA, someone recommended I read *The Success Principles* by Jack Canfield. After I read that book, I was asking myself questions I hadn't asked before or for a really long time.

What is my life purpose?

What makes me happy?

What used to make me happy?

By Jenée Dana

66

I realized that I wasn't fulfilled. I actually enjoyed my job. I was a beauty consultant, and I got to play makeup with girls all day. I was having a lot of fun, so I didn't understand why I felt like something was missing, until I started thinking about and answering those questions. Each time I came up with an answer, I would just take one step towards that answer and see what happened. That process led me to take my mom on her dream trip to Alaska. My mom's #1 Bucket List item was to go to Alaska, dog sled, and see the auroras after reading books like *White Fang* by Jack London. I set up the entire trip, from learning to drive our own dog sled, taking a sled ride at night to see the aurora's (unfortunately, it was too cloudy that night), and having a majestic helicopter ride where we got to land on a glacier! It was amazing. My mom told me, "Jenee, thank you so much. That was the trip of a life time, and I will never ever forget that helicopter ride."

I already knew I loved to travel with family and friends, but I realized right then and there that I LOVE to see others check off items on their Bucket List. Seeing her eyes light up made my eyes light up too. Those memories are what life is all about! Then I went to a retreat called One Great Goal with Ursula Mentjes, and I narrowed my purpose down even further. To me, checking an item off my Bucket List by myself is just an accomplishment, but having an amazing Bucket List experience with family or friends is a memory that will last a lifetime. My first mission and purpose is to help 10 million people check off at least one item on their bucket list with their family and friends.

Then I joined a book mastermind with my book coach Amanda Johnson. During the process of planning my book, I realized who I wanted to work with. I work best with students, parents of those students, entrepreneurs and sales professionals. I get energy from working with these groups and positive, nice people. If I hadn't started writing this book, it might have taken me longer to figure out who I am passionate about working with. Let's face it. You don't want to work with everyone - even in business. Some people are just draining and awful to be around. Stick with the people and activities that bring you happiness and joy.

By Jenée Dana

What am
I wired to do?

Exercise

Part 1: Have Fun & Get It Done

1. Think back to your childhood when you would get caught for running around the house with your underwear or wearing it on your head. (C'mon, every kid does that, right?) If you can't remember your childhood, think back to high school (when running around in your underwear in public was not a good idea).

What did you love to do?
(list 5-10 things)

2. What do you love to do now? Or what are you doing when you feel like that little kid with endless energy, running around with undies on their head again? (list 5-10 things)

3. Name a few instances when you remember having SO MUCH FUN that you didn't notice your undies riding up.

What were you doing?

Where were you?

Who were you with?

What about that event/
time made it fun?

4. Are you a "one leg at a time" or "two feet in" type of person? What are your natural trengths/skills?

What comes easily to you? (Put a star next to your top 2)

Examples: really good at math, can speak in front of groups, pull a team together and finish a project, amazing eye for color and undertones, etc.

5. What does your underwear say about you? Is it FUN, practical, color-coordinated, strewn all over your room, or carefully organized in your drawer?

What are my best personality characteristics? (Put a star next to your top 2)

Examples: Exuberance, Creativity, Fun, Leader, Diligent, Loving, Funny, etc.

6. If your underwear gave you super powers whenever you put them on, how would you use your super-undies to make the world a better, more fun place?

What do I love to do for others?

Examples: To make people laugh so hard they pee their pants; to inspire others to live to their full potential; bring a smile to someone's face, etc.

What do you want others to have? Not just those you love, but everyone.

Examples: happiness, abundance of wealth and love, peace, bucket list experiences with family and friends, a home they love to live in, purpose, health, etc.

7. How could your undie-skills and personality aid in making the world a better, more fun place to be?

(Hint: What best personality characteristics and strengths/skills can contribute to what you want others to have?)

8. How do you choose your undies? Do you prefer certain brands over others? Comfort over price? Look over comfort?

What do you value? (Prioritize your list, making 1 the most important and so on. When prioritizing, think "I want both, but if I had to choose, I would rather have _____.")

Examples: Loyalty, integrity, family, honesty, quality time, recognition, service (both given and received), touch (hugs and kisses from those we love), gifts, relationships, money, health, spirituality and faith, career, accomplishments, personal growth, fun, etc.

By Jenée Dana

9. Are you happy with what you see when you open up your underwear drawer?

Are you currently doing what you love and value?

And/Or are you currently making a living doing what you love doing?

If not, how can you create a living doing what you love? Just brainstorm and write down all thoughts that come to mind, no matter how ridiculous they might seem.

Example: I know someone who loves to read and write. She also loves to go to the spa. She has a business that gives retreats at spas to help authors write their books.

10. When you leave this earth, how do you want people to remember you (besides someone who had some stylin' undies)?

Part 2:
Gracefully Remove Your
Wedgie = Wedgiefication

According to Urbandictionary.com wedgiefication is defined as: "When you are having a wedgie and you want to be wedgie free, you go through a process called 'Wedgiefication', where you free yourself from a wedgie."

1. Which undies are in the "never wear again" pile because they don't fit right, give you a wedgie, or are just plain worn out?

What do you really NOT like to do? What activities are you currently doing that do not make you happy?

2. Pick your wedgie.

Pick one thing you don't like to do that you are willing to remove and replace with something you love to do (from part 1) this week.

Note: If you still feel a little fuzzy on your life purpose, no worries. It took me a few times of doing these exercises before it became crystal clear. Others get it right away. Everyone is different.

By Jenée Dana

I chose to walk off the traditional path and graduate early. Monica got four degrees in 5 years, two of them being master's degrees. Danny could have graduated in 3 years, but he decided the 4-year path was better for him. Each of our paths was right for us. Do what you think is right for *you*.

Are you (do you want to be) involved in clubs or organizations in college? What kind?

Do you want internships in your field of study?

Will you go to grad school?

Do you love, like, eh...I don't really care, or hate what you are studying?

Do midterms and finals stress you out?

Are midterms and finals not stressful because you love the subject?

Do you want to travel? Possibly live in another country for a few months to a year?

Are you happy?

Yes = woo hoo! No = What makes you happy?

Based on all of your answers to the questions I've included, which way are you leaning? Look over your answers about what you love to do and your "I Call DIBS" (goals), when you want to achieve them, and where you want to live when you are going to school. What options feel right to you? Is the 3-year possibility even doable in your mind right now?

Follow your heart, listen to your gut, and move towards the things that excite you and make you happy. Do what you are wired to do. You may hear warnings from friends or adults that want to protect you because they don't want to see you fail or be disappointed. But success comes from 99% failure. The other person that it didn't work out for either quit too soon or realized that it wasn't their path or passion.

Chapter 4

Get From Here to There & Keep Your Underwear

Create Your Plan

> "By failing to prepare,
> you are preparing to fail."
>
> *Benjamin Franklin*

How is it even possible?

Note: Feel free to skip over sections that do not apply to you. It is not my goal in life to make you read a bunch of worthless material you don't need *(unlike some college professors I had)*.

Option A (for high school students)

Take AP (Advanced Placement) courses and pass required tests with the score of 3/4/5 to get college units and waive requirements.

You're taking classes in high school anyway, and if you don't pass the AP test, it doesn't affect your regular high school grade. You could get an A in the class and fail the AP test, and you would still keep your A in the class. So it doesn't hurt you to take the test. But, if you pass the test, you get college credits.

I passed my AP US history test by the skin of my teeth, but I still got eight units and a couple requirements waived at UCLA because of it. My friend Katie, who also graduated UCLA in three years, came into UCLA with 28 units and got requirements waived because she passed a few AP tests. Danny also had 28 units entering UCLA.

If you're not in AP classes yet, talk to your high school counselor and get them on your class schedule.

Option B (high school students)
Take general education requirements classes at the local junior college while you are in high school.

Community college costs less than regular college (to a certain extent) and, depending on your parents' income level, your classes there might even be free. Sometimes the junior college (JC) professor will surprise you and give you a really hard class, but generally speaking, JC classes are not much harder than high school classes, and you get your general education requirements out of the way. Why make life harder, especially for classes you normally don't care about?

You can take these classes during the summer or during the school year. **Joint enrollment** allows you to leave campus for college classes and get credit for high school class at the same time. I am all about being efficient and "killing two birds with one stone," especially if it's an annoying bird. (**Note:** No birds were harmed in the making of my college experience or this book.)

By Jenée Dana

Find the general education requirements list at each of your top five university choices' websites. Your college counselor can also help you with verifying this information. Compare the university lists with the available classes at your local junior college. Talk to your high school counselor, college counselor at the junior college, and the counselor at your college of choice. Make sure to get it in writing from the college of choice that the class is transferable.

I don't believe in the myth that you need to focus on your weaknesses and overcome them in order to feel accomplished in life. If there is a general education (GE) class subject that you know you don't like you have somes options so you have more time and energy to focus on your strengths.

1. Get it out of the way at a junior college
2. Find a professor that gets rave reviews from most their students
3. Find a professor that is rated easy by their students

Option C (college students)

Take more classes every quarter/semester.

In a quarter system, three classes usually accounts for a full load.

During my first two years at UCLA, I was afraid to overwhelm myself and take too many units because I was already stressed out with the measly bare minimum 12 units. I didn't know what I was doing without the life management tools and study strategies included later in this book. However, when put under pressure, I cook fast, and I figured it out.

"Please read the study and life management chapters, so you can take an extra class and not feel so overwhelmed and, most importantly, still have a life."

4 units per class X 3 = 12 units

If you take just one more class per quarter...

4 classes X 4 units = 16 units

12 unit quarter	16 units quarter
12	16
X 3 quarters	X 3 quarters
36 units	48 units
before summer school	before summer school

48 units

-36 units

12 unit difference

By taking one extra class each
quarter for three quarters, you
could add almost two extra
full-time quarters worth of units
to your school year without having
to take any summer school.

Note: I used the quarter system for this example. If you are going to a college with a semester system, just apply the same logic to the semester unit requirements.

Option D (college students)

Add summer school and/or winter break classes to your class schedule.

Most schools divide the summer into two or three sessions. College students usually take one or two classes during a summer school session. If you don't mind just plowing through, you can take one to two classes during each session offered.

Personally, I like my summer breaks and winter vacations, so I took most of them off. However, I attended summer school one session before my freshman year because it was required by the Freshman Studies Program (FSP) and Academic Advancement Program (AAP). Then, after my sophomore year, when I decided to do two years of college in one, I took a couple summer school classes before my third year and one class after my third year.

2 classes = 8 units

3 summer sessions x 8 units = 24 units

24 units = 2 full time quarters

2 full time quarters = 2/3 of a school
year done in 1 summer

By Jenée Dana

A summer school class can last anywhere from three to six weeks. So instead of studying for 10 weeks, you cover a lot of ground in about half the time. Depending on the professor, most often there is less material covered in the shorter time-frame. However, don't always count on this. Some professors look at summer as a way to cover more ground in less time.

Ratemyprofessors.com is something that I used in college to see what other college students had to say about a particular teacher when signing up for classes. It has gotten even better since then with more reviews. Use it to know who the good professors are, and avoid the ones who have already proven to be boring and ineffective.

If you are not good at foreign language, and your university thinks that foreign language should be taken every single day of the week, I highly recommend taking your foreign language requirements in the summer. Do not make the same mistake I did!

I had to commute from home to UCLA on the 405 freeway during my sophomore year Monday, Tuesday, Wednesday, Thursday and, oh yes, Friday. Because of the awful LA traffic and the van-pool, I had to leave my home at 5:30am and I left UCLA around 5:00pm, only to be stuck in traffic for more than two hours and arrive home around 7:30pm every day. This might be the average LA county worker's commute....but not a college student's. ☹ Needless to say,

I took a lot of naps in the library and tried to get all my studying done while I was on campus so I could relax at home.

If you don't want to take extra classes during the quarter or semester, Option D is a great way for you to get more units and classes out of the way. A sucky option, in my opinion, but an option nonetheless.

Option E (college students)

If you are fluent in a foreign language, you can double major with that language.

It looks good on resumes for companies that are looking for bilingual employees and, let's be real – it's an easy way to keep up your grade point average. You can also take tests to waive class requirements in the major. Depending on the school, you can still get credits towards your graduation or at least have the class requirement shown as complete.

Option F (college students)

Take as many classes as you can that overlap in your college requirements.

If you are already sure about your major, take a course that will satisfy both the general education requirements AND your major requirements at the same time. If you want to double major, find courses within your majors that overlap, or find majors with many courses that overlap. It's possible!

What do you
want to major in?

Woud you like to double or triple major?

Is there a related major
with a lot of overlapping classes?

This makes obtaining a double or
even triple major much easier.

Option G (college students)
Double LOAD!

I don't know what came over me. I went from being stressed out with 12 units a quarter to wanting to take 26 units a quarter to graduate that year. I guess I don't blame some people for thinking I had lost my mind. Thank God I did it though, because in doing so, I realized what I was really capable of and how to get more done without feeling overwhelmed.

Why would *you* choose the double load?

If you're like me and decide things on a whim, you might find yourself at the end of your sophomore year wanting to graduate the following year.

You might actually function better with a double load. You can get more done in less time because you don't have time to just sit and fart around. It scares me to think of how much time I spent just *thinking* about what I had to do my freshman and sophomore years... and that is what was stressing me out the most – the "thinking about it", not the "getting it done". When you're really busy and don't have time to think about it, you just do it.

Finally, if you take a double load your sophomore year, you might keep your options open for graduating early, and/or getting a double or triple degree. Get permission from your college counselor and from the Dean to take more than 19 units per quarter or your maximum units for the semester.

Big Hairy BUTTs

Even the best laid out plans can be met with obstacles. The following are questions I've heard from students experiencing some challenges. When you know what you are up against, solutions are easier to come by.

By Jenée Dana

BUTT what if the class I need is impacted?

E-mail the professor and find out when they are going to be in their office prior to the first class. Show up and plead your case. Surprisingly, most college students are not going to take the time to do this, and it will give you a much better shot at getting into the class. Professors like students who take initiative and really want to be in their class. There will be a few students who are registered in the class but don't show up on the first day. And if you show up, and he has you on the waiting list, you will likely bump off the lazy kid who didn't show up the first day of school. Sucks for them.

BUTT what if classes are NOT offered this quarter or semester or summer?

See if the local junior college or private university offers it. Yes, private universities will cost more, but it is one class, and you will get it out of the way.

Verify that the class requirement and units will transfer AND make sure you get it in writing on letterhead or through e-mail from the college counselor at your university and the college counselor from the college where you are taking the extra class.

BUTT what if my major is impacted?

Remember Monica's strategy in Chapter 3? She went to a private university that had a joint program with University of California Irvine in order to get two degrees in 5 years rather than the planned 6 years for one degree because the Engineering major at UCI was impacted. While her plans changed along the way, Monica always took quick action on finding the best and quickest solution.

Is your brain on overload yet with all these options? The tips and strategies in this chapter are not the only way to graduate early — just *most* of the ways. They worked for me and other highly successful students. Try them! They do work. Also, don't forget to get creative. The possibilities are endless.

Part 2

What's In Your Undie Drawer?

Tips and Tools for Getting Good Grades and Enjoying Your Social Life

> "A good system shortens
> the road to the goal."

Orison Swett Marden

Many of the tips and tools you will gain from the following chapters will transfer from college, to your career, to your everyday life. Everything from how to reach your goals, or like I say "how to call DIBS on what you want," to how to manage your time and study efficiently so you get great grades and still have time for fun, to dealing with crazy roommates, can be applied to future adventures and relationships.

Have you ever had a class that if your life depended on it, you could not explain how it had any application to your life or the real world? I have had plenty of those. So I am going to explain to you why each of the following topics is important and how it applies to your everyday life.

Why should I call DIBS on what I want?

This is most commonly known as goal-setting, but I like to call DIBS because I am claiming what I want versus reaching for a goal that may seem far away. I learned this from Glenn Morshower, an actor on the show *24* and the movie *Transformers,* who you will learn more about in the next chapter.

I Call DIBS
Done In Bold Steps

First, you need to claim what you want:
"I call DIBS", and then take action and get it Done In Bold Steps.

Which options sound best to you right now? Why?

What is your first step (DIBS) toward making this happen?

Ex: talking to your counselor about what requirements overlap, investigating your top 5 universities, etc.

By Jenée Dana

In life, if you ask for nothing, you get nothing. So, be clear on what you want and ask for it. When you call DIBS on what you want, you are more likely to get it.

You already have a goal (DIBS) to graduate from college; otherwise you wouldn't be reading this book.

How does time management apply to me?

Time management actually does not exist. Time management really is a high sense of what your *values* and *priorities* are. When you spend time on only what you value, most of your time feels like *free-time*. Do you value going out with friends, playing sports, or watching TV? There is no wrong answer.

Does time go away after school? Ha! Ha! NO! You will need to know your values and priorities in regular life, maybe even more than you'll need them in college. Highly productive people earn promotions or grow businesses faster than others. And when you CREATE time to relax and have fun through your values and priorities system, it makes your work week more productive.

How are study skills going to relate to me after school?

Many of the skills you learn for studying (like the 80% rule) can help you out when memorizing and preparing for a big presentation at work. If you learn how to learn fast, you'll get ahead fast in whatever environment you find yourself in.

How does being social and networking relate to me after school?

This is one of the most important aspects of life! Family and friends are what life is all about. "No man ever said on his deathbed, 'I wish I spent more time in the office,'" said Former Senator Paul Tsongas's friend when he decided to resign from his position after being diagnosed with cancer. If you don't have love and relationships, you have nothing.

The connections you make with *like-minded* people in high school, college, and throughout life, are not only going to add to your FUN, but they can also become a great network to lean on when you need it. In return, you're there to support them when they do. You never know how you can help your friend in the future or how they will help you.

Relationship-building is also key to being successful in work environments and when growing your own business. People hire and promote people they like. Of course you have to be competent and qualified for the job, but think about it, how hard is it to work with a sour old turd? Same goes for business. People buy from people they like. How often do you give money to someone you hate? Or a company you hate? Sooner or later, you will look for someone or a company you like. It is important to build relationships and not be a turd to be around. Make sure your attitude doesn't stink or people will avoid the smell.

So if this all makes sense to you, ye shall pass to Chapter 5.

By Jenée Dana

Chapter 5

Maple Syrup in Your Shoes or Corn Flakes in Your Undies...You Pick

Call DIBS and Get What You Want

> "For those of you that think the odds are against you. You swam the fastest out of 180 to 400 million other swimmers just to get on this planet!"
>
> *Glenn Morshower*

There are a million books that tell you how to reach your goals or call your DIBS, but this is the only one that tells you how to do that and still have fun.

There are things that we all need to survive in this life (food, water, shelter, and money to pay for these) and then there are things that we want (to own hot rides, experience true love, be healthy, develop a connection with a higher being / God, have an awesome career, feel happy, give back, leave a legacy). Whether you need "it" or want "it", there are the ways that most people get "it", and then there are the ways that *really successful people* get "it".

Really successful people – not just wealthy people, but Olympic athletes, political leaders, etc. – all end up in the top 3% through a specific process of calling DIBS on what they want and working strategically to achieve them.

When you ask for nothing, guess what you get? *Nothing!* That's why it's so important for you to know what you want.

Now, some of you reading this book have some really serious DIBS – get through college as fast as you can, create your own business, build a non-profit, find a cure for cancer, etc. while others may be thinking, "But I'm only 18 years old. How am I supposed to know what I want?"

For those of you who already have serious DIBS, this chapter will help you take the "bigness" and "difficulty" out of them by being strategic in how you will accomplish them.

For those of you who don't have that direction yet, chill-ax! You have time. BUT take your time with this chapter and consider all of the questions and do all of the exercises. Who knows? By the time you finish, you may have some DIBS and a great way to achieve them. ☺

So, what do you want?

"Success on MY Terms" is an exercise in the *My Focus Book* planner. It helps you to really clarify what you want in nine different areas of your life. I am including this exercise for you here with explanations of each of the areas to help you either figure it out or gain even more clarity on what your *true* priorities are.

Faith & Spirituality

Whatever your faith or beliefs are, it is important to be in tune with them. Don't worry; I am not here to preach and especially not to judge. You may have a different idea or opinions on the subject of faith, and that is a-okay. The point is, really think about what you want your faith and spirituality to mean to you.

There are so many distractions in our world today; it can be easy to stray from what we believe in our core and begin to feel conflicted, frustrated and/or stressed.

Finding the time to pray and/or meditate helps release stress and worry. All the answers to our problems are within, I believe, because God put them there a long time ago, and we just have to stop and truly listen to find them.

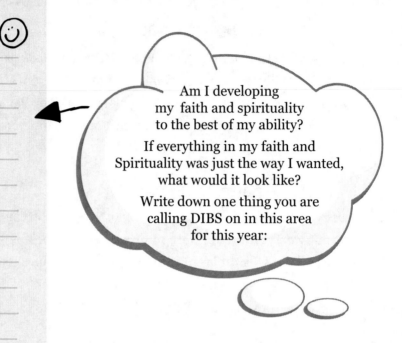

Am I developing
my faith and spirituality
to the best of my ability?

If everything in my faith and
Spirituality was just the way I wanted,
what would it look like?

Write down one thing you are
calling DIBS on in this area
for this year:

Family

Family is so important. Most of my family is weird, and many of them did not provide a good example for me to follow. Well, I guess the good example was how *not* to be, whether it was drugs, lack of responsibility, or just plain lack of character. You might have a similar type of family, or worse. No worries – I've learned that we can choose who we spend our time with, and we can choose who our family is too. I believe that blood is not the only thing that binds families together. I am blessed to be surrounded by my mom, my future in-laws, and friends that I consider to be my real family. A family

By Jenée Dana

loves and supports us and doesn't break into our houses when we're on vacation (yeah, that really happened). So think about what family means to you and what you want it to feel like.

Am I making my family feel loved and appreciated to the best of my ablitity?

How do I envision these relationships?

If everything in my family life were just the way I wanted, what would it look like?

Write down one thing you are calling DIBS on in this area for this year:

Career/School

We all spend about a third of our lives in school or at work, so it's important to figure out what is going to make us happy there. Otherwise, kiss approximately 23 years of your life goodbye, because that's how long you are going to be miserable.

> Am I doing
> what I love?
>
> Am I where I want to be in
> my school career?
>
> Am I valuing my time efficiently and
> accomplishing what I want in school?
>
> If everything about school were just he way
> I wanted, what would it look like?
>
> If everything about my future
> career were just the way I wanted,
> what would it look like?

Personal Growth

Have you ever heard the old proverb, "You can't fill a cup that is already full"? It's a total cliché but true. I hate to break it to you, but we never ever stop learning in life. Well, hopefully we don't. The day we stop learning is the day we start dying. So try and be open to new experiences. Learning is not always found in a textbook. It is found in real life experiences, watching Bear Grylls on TV survive in the wilderness, traveling to other countries, and even talking with friends.

By Jenée Dana

Do I love ME?

If I can't love myself, how will I
ever be able to do things for MYSELF?
How will I fully love others?

How do I want to be remembered?

Am I eliminating bad habits by creating new
positive habits?

What do I want to learn?

What skills do I want to acquire?

What would I look like...

If everything about me was just the way I
wanted, who would I be?

How would I act?

How would I treat others? As Glenn
Morshower says, "It is in my nature to be
_____" and he fills in the blank
with how he wants to be.

Write down one thing you are calling
DIBS on in this area for
this year:

Health (Emotional/Mental/Physical)

Sometimes we give so much of ourselves to others
and ignore our personal needs. Then we look at
ourselves and we don't even know who we are

anymore. If you can't take care of yourself, how do you expect to take care of others? I love Glenn Morshower's perspective on this. Your body is the trophy you won against 5 million other competitors (i.e. tadpoles) in the initial race to conception. You will have it every day of your life and it is the vehicle of life. So if you don't take care of that, there is really no point in taking care of anything.

Am I taking care of myself to the best of my ability?

How do I handle difficult situations?

How do I want to handle them?

Am I in control of my emotions?

Do I give my body the nourishment and care it needs and deserves?

If everything about my health (emotional/mental/ physical) were just the way I wanted, what would I look like?

How would I feel?

Write down one thing you are calling DIBS on in this area for this year:

By Jenée Dana

Lifetime Funding

Money does not buy happiness, but it sure does buy choices! Don't be afraid of money. Some people reject the idea of being wealthy because they fear they may become greedy or selfish. Some feel guilt because other people don't have that much. Have you ever said "Uck! What a waste of money!" when someone wealthier than you bought a toy for themselves? The way I see it, they've worked hard to reach their level of wealth, and they can spend their money however they want. When I am ready to work that hard and/or take a risk on myself like they did, I'll have those things too.

And you can do a lot more good with tithing (giving to charity) from a larger paycheck rather than just sitting around and thinking about "those poor people".

I had a relative once say, "Why should I make a lot of money when poor kids in East LA don't even have shoes?" To which my grandma replied, "You feel bad because some kids don't have shoes? What good is it for you to sit around and complain about it? If you care so much, go make a lot of money so you can go buy those kids some shoes!!!" Any amount of tithing to good causes is great. Don't be ashamed of your current paycheck. However, tithing 10% of 5 million is a lot more than 10% of $50,000. Am I right? You can do more good with more money.

Am I creating a
budget that includes giving,
saving, investing and spending?

How do I want to fund my life?

If my finances could be as much as I want,
how much money would I have?

How much do I want to make daily,
monthly, yearly?

What would I spend it on?

Write down one thing you are
calling DIBS on in this area
for this year:

Relationships & Circle of Influence

You are like, or become like, those who you spend the most time with!!! Be careful and selective of who you let into your backyard, figuratively and literally. Remember what we talked about earlier? Stay away from TROLLS! They suck the energy out of you. You have a choice to be around crappy people or happy people. Choose to be around those that inspire you, support you, love you and make you feel good, and dump the rest like you did your ex.

By Jenée Dana

Who are the five
people I hang around the most?

Are they positive, negative or neither?

If I could hang out with an ideal type of
person, what type of person would I want to
be associated with?

If my relationships could be exactly the way I
wanted, how would they be?

If my circle of influence could be
exactly the way I wanted,
who would they be?

Write down one thing you are
calling DIBS on in this area
for this year:

Fun

It is sooooooooooooooooooooooooooo important to have fun. I can't *stress* it enough! (LOL!) When you are having fun, you have more energy and are generally a happier person, right? Ever been to Disneyland or any other amusement park? Especially when you were little, you couldn't sleep the night before because you were so excited about the next day. And the next day at the park, you were having so much fun that you didn't even remember you were sleep deprived.

Some people think that as soon as you become an adult, fun goes out the window. Let me just say, I think those people are crazy. Yes, adult life does come with additional responsibility, but there are certain aspects of childhood we should never let go of, and the number one most important thing to hold on to is FUN. Sure, the way you have fun might change over the years as your values, preferences, and priorities shift. If your eyes have not lit up in awhile, it is time to reevaluate what you are doing. When you know what makes your heart smile, try and figure out a way to do more of it.

When was the last time I had fun?

What fun activities do I enjoy that I'd like to do more of?

What looks like fun that I have not tried yet?

What activities do I want to pursue on my own and what activities do I want to pursue with friends and/or family?

If my fun time could be anything I wanted, what would it be?

Write down one thing you are calling DIBS on in this area for this year:

By Jenée Dana

Giving Back

Giving back to your community and the world is an awesome experience. Helping others not only can change their lives, but yours will be changed in the process. An immense amount of personal growth takes place with every giving experience. What you put into the lives of others comes back to you tenfold. There are different ways to give back. One is tithing roughly 10 % of your income to a charity that means something to you. It could be for cancer research, saving the rain forest, feeding the hungry, or any other need out there. Even right now, whether you have part time job, or allowance money – consider donating 10%, even if it is just $1. It will help you form a good habit for the future. If you don't have money to donate or prefer not to, you can still give back with your time. Volunteer for local organizations or charities that inspire you.

What cause is important to me?

How do I want to give back – volunteering, tithing, or both?

If I could give any amount I want to any charities I want, how much would I give?

Write down one thing you are calling DIBS on in this area for this year:

www.myfocusbook.com

Call DIBS on What You Want

When I interviewed Glenn Morshower, actor on shows like *24* and in movies like *Transformers* and other summer blockbusters, he shared amazing strategies on how to get what you want.

I took the claim analogy a little further and came up with "I call DIBS!" Have you ever called dibs on the last slice of pizza? You called dibs, and claimed it as your slice and no one else's.

By Jenée Dana

Goal vs. It's My Nature

If you've been kind of pissy to others lately, instead of saying, "It's my goal to be kind," you might want to consider saying, "It's my nature to be kind." Meaning kindness is who I am. Decency is who I am. Love is who I am. Is it my goal to achieve all sorts of things in life, including a successful show business career? No, it's my nature.

The moment we shift from something being our goal to it being in our nature, it becomes eminently have-able. When you say, "It's my nature to be _____", there is not a question in your mind as to whether or not it can be done. You were born that way (as Lady Gaga would attest to!). The only reason you don't have your goal at the moment, is because you have not been behaving as though it was in your nature. When you behave like what you want is in your nature, you get what you want.

Glenn Morshower

Here are some general guidelines for calling out your DIBS and getting what you want:

SO, HOW WILL YOU ACHIEVE IT?

Create a Clear Picture
(DIBS Poster)

This may sound silly to most of you. Just know that you're not alone. When I was first introduced to a goal/DIBS poster my freshman year in high school, I thought my teacher Mr. Cortez was insane. "You are telling me that if I draw and color on this white piece of paper exactly what I want for my high school career that at the end of four years I should have most, if not all, of it? Yeah right, crazy." I only made the goal poster because it was a homework assignment, and I would get points towards my grade.

Four years later, I'd completely forgotten about the school poster until I found myself opening an envelope and wondering why I was getting a letter addressed to me by someone that writes a lot like me. (I had addressed it to myself four years before as part of the assignment.) When I opened the envelope and saw my goal poster, I was in shock.

I had achieved every single thing on the poster that I had said I wanted to do or have in high school. I had drawn a road map on the poster, and along the road, I had drawn a piece of paper with squiggly lines on it in and an A+ at the top. I was graduating with an above A+ grade point average. I had also drawn symbols that represented varsity sports, and I joined two varsity teams in high school.

Embarrassingly enough, there was also a little crown along the road that symbolized being a Homecoming Princess. I didn't care about being Queen – all I wanted to do was wear a pretty dress and tiara and ride around the football track in the 1930s car, sitting on top of

By Jenée Dana

the back seat like a Kennedy. *(Permission to laugh granted.)* My grandma used to be the secretary at my high school, and when I was five, she took me to a homecoming game, and I saw the princesses drive around in the old cars around the track all decked out. At five years old I had my first goal – to be a princess.

The most surprising part of my goal poster was that at the end of the road, I had drawn a Bruin with the UCLA logo underneath. To be honest, I didn't even like UCLA at the time. I was so sick of the banter between USC and UCLA that I did not care about either school. But at fourteen years old, I knew I would need to go to college, and not knowing which college I wanted to go to, I just drew the first college that popped in my head. I was accepted to UCLA my senior year, which was the year they had the highest number of applicants in their history. Wow, right?

Being crystal clear on what you want and calling out specific DIBS is important; and even if it's hard for you to take the process seriously, do it. You never know. Maybe it will all happen like mine did!

Chunk It Down

Start with that big picture (end result) in mind and then work your way backwards, chunking down that BIG GOAL into bite-size pieces.

When you think about it, college already does this for you. You start with the end result in mind of getting your bachelor of arts or bachelor of science degree. Then they chunk it down for you by quarter or semester. Colleges give you a general idea about how many classes or units you will need to take each quarter or semester in order to graduate in four years. When I was in college, all I did was reorganize the chunking down of the goal to fit my productivity style. Instead of taking the recommended 12 units to graduate in 4 years, I took 26 units to graduate in 3 at the last minute. I just ADJUSTED the amount of work to fit the time-frame I wanted. You can do this with any DIBS/goal.

$$\frac{\text{Your "I call DIBS" or Goal}}{\text{Amount of time to finish DIBS or Goal}} = \text{Chunking It Down}$$

Use a Planner

If you are not already using a calendar planner, I suggest you go get one. Right about now, I will shamelessly insert a plug for the calendar planner that I have created called *My Focus Book*. The online version is free at www.myfocusbook.com or you can purchase a paper planner at www.havefunandgetitdone.com. You can use whatever planner you want; just make sure you're at least using something.

Paper planners are generally better than the electronic calendars in your phone, especially for the visual and kinesthetic learner. When I open up my phone calendar and just see a bunch of little dots, it drives me up the wall. What do all those dots *mean*?

By Jenée Dana

I can't see anything. But when I open up my paper planner, I can see all my due dates and projects and appointments right away.

Now, if you are using a tablet with a larger screen, you could argue that an electronic planner is just as useful, and it can be. In fact, as I write this, I'm designing the online app version of *My Focus Book*. It will allow college students and professionals to call DIBS on what they want and go get it, while still having a life. If you are not willing to invest in a tablet, I suggest just getting a paper planner that will cost you anywhere from $15-$100 depending on the type you get.

Write your DIBS/goals in your planner. ➤

Write down all the due dates on the syllabus that your professor gives you in your Monthly Calendar tab, and don't forget to jot down a list of 100 things you want to do before you die in your Bucket List tab. Bucket list experiences with family and friends are what makes life worth living. So while you are planning your schooling, take some time to think about what fun and amazing experiences you want to have before you kick the bucket.

Everything I Want To Accomplish, Aquire, & Become Before I Kick The Bucket

1   Be on the Ellen Show as a guest

2   Visit every continent

3   Own an island

4   Get paid $100,000 to speak for 2 hours (free first class accommodations for me and family all over the world)

5   Vacation homes in Spain and Germany

6   Personal home with country feel, within 15 to 30 minutes of the beach (to ovoid beach overcast)

7   Marry the person I am going to spend the rest of my life with (an amazing, caring, sweet, funny, responsible, smart, best friend)

8   Female billionaire by 29 years old

9   Own white BMW with tan leather seating!

10   ~~Fly in a helicopter~~

11   ~~Land on Alaskan glacier in helicopter~~

12   ~~Drive my own dogsled in Alaska (4 dogs)~~

13   Get paid to go on luxury cruises with family or friends all over the world

14   Pet wild whales in San Ignacio Bay, Baja Ca

15   ~~Kiss Blarney Stone in Ireland~~

16   #1 Amazon Best seller 'Have Fun & Get It Done: Graduate From a Top University in 3 Years or Less'

17   Oscar for Best Actress (...you never know)

By Jenée Dana

October 2011

Monday	Tuesday	Wednesday	Thursday
3 Outline Comm Paper	4 Outline Workshop	5 Outline Geog Paper	6 Write Comm Paper
10 Study M/T	11 Study M/T	12 9am Psych M/T 12pmComm M/T	13 12pm Geog M/T 2pm Edu M/T
17 Revise Comm Paper Write Geog Paper	18 Practice Workshop Outline Psych Paper	19 12pmComm Paper Practice Workshop	20 2pm Edu Workshop
24 Revise Psych Paper	25 Revise Geog Paper	26 9am Psych Paper	27 12pm Geog Paper
31			

Friday	Saturday	Sunday	I call DIBS
			A's on M/T's
			A's on papers
			A on W/shop
			Done In Bold Steps
3	4	5	- Outline Papers
	FUN	FUN/REST	-Outline Workshop
MOVIE NIGHT			-Revise paper
			-Practice Workshop
10	11	12	-Study for Midterms
Mini ROAD TRIP	Mini ROAD TRIP	Mini ROAD TRIP	
17	18	19	Notes
Write Geog Paper Football Game	FUN	FUN/REST	
24	25	26	
		FUN/REST	
HOT DATE	Halloween Party		

By Jenée Dana

Then chunk down those goals. If the paper is due on the 25th, make a rough draft due date for yourself for the 16th, leaving plenty of room for revision. *Do what you know works for you.* Depending on your style, you may like to write one small bit at a time, or you may prefer to write it all in one sitting. For the person who prefers a small bit at a time, you could give yourself due dates for the outline and write one paragraph each day. Those who like to write all at once can just schedule a writing day for an outline, and a writing day for the rough draft, and a writing day for the final revisions. Or you can write it all the night before, as long as you get it done before it is due.

Identify FIVE Done In Bold Steps (DIBS) a day. If you do not have daily sheets in your planner, then you need to write down your five DIBS on the appropriate day in your weekly calendar. You can see an example of how you want to fill out your Weekly Calendar and your My Values & Priorities (MVP) Week in Chapter 6.

When you're in college, your main goal is to graduate. So your daily goals include your homework and studying. However, you can have other goals too, like to go skydiving with friends, complete a project that helps inner city students, or lose the "Freshman 15". When you complete at least five Done In Bold Steps every day, you move really quickly towards what you want.

Don't Forget to Have Fun

The reason I interviewed Glenn Morshower is because I believe he is the epitome of 'Have Fun & Get It Done'. He still plays like a kid, and he is very successful in his career because of it.

One day, I listened to an idea and put maple syrup in my shoes before an audition. And not just a little maple syrup...a LOT of maple syrup! You could hear the "squish, squish, squish" as I walked down the halls. I ended up passing the audition and getting a really great acting role.

Then I wanted to take it a step up and used the produce section at the grocery store as my playground. For every audition, I have either put bologna in my underpants or some other type of food product somewhere, and I get every role.

Why does it work? Syrup in your shoes is certainly not the typical use for syrup. Wouldn't you agree? People usually put in on pancakes, waffles, or chicken, but it tends to end there. But what if you put it in your shoes? Wouldn't you at least feel different? You would probably feel great. You would probably even feel funny.

By Jenée Dana

When I told my wife that I wanted to put syrup in my shoes, she was so supportive, she pulled two brands out of the cupboard and asked me what kind without hesitation. We started putting the syrup in my shoes and we were both smiling. Then when I put them on, I felt like I was 6 years old— so youthful, so free, so non-traditional, and so happy. The list goes on and on about how different you feel when you fill your shoes with syrup and put them on. You don't just feel stupid, you feel daring. You know? Like I dared to do this. I bet you I am the only person in Southern California, or even the world, that at this moment is standing in syrup and loving it. I am probably one of the few in history to have ever done it. I know for a fact I am not the only one now because several have written me and told me that it changed their perception on what used to be regarded as a heavy or intimidating experience. Now they understand how to dis-empower the heaviness, or fear factor, when going into a job audition or being nervous about a first date. You opt to put little marshmallows between your toes or cornflakes in your underpants. About the time you start to get nervous, just wiggle your toes and remember you have marshmallows between them... and it's not going to be a problem.

The bottom line is it works and I am a big advocate of doing things in life that work. I don't care how mainstream they are or how strange and peculiar they are. There is one big rule that I have. If what you are doing works AND does not hurt anyone, then do it!

If it hurts someone, you are breaking the rules. But last time I checked, putting bologna in your underwear hurts no one.

By Jenée Dana

It's not just about doing some weird thing. That is what a closed and judgmental person would think of it as. All they would think is, "Oh gosh, that is just childish." They don't realize that their problem is their need be judgmental of something that might just set them free if they were to try it.

So many decisions adults make are based on other people's opinions. But when we are kids, we kind of just do what occurs to us. Adults think they have graduated, but they have actually moved backwards into believing that whatever they do has to be a certain way so no one will disapprove of it. We end up losing our uniqueness in the equation. It is a shame for people to lose their uniqueness and the divine purpose for which they were created. I do not believe any two people are exactly alike and that is why you needed to be created. The world had not seen you yet. And I don't mean just the physical you, I mean your mission. Whatever your mission is, it's an unparalleled mission. You are here in the world for reasons not yet seen by another human being. And if you don't follow your mission, you not only rob yourself of being able to experience that life, you rob the rest of the world of what we were supposed to experience—you walking in your own light. If you don't live the life you were designed to live, the whole world misses out.

The minute you stop being playful, you are in trouble. That is when the aging process really starts accelerating. We certainly live happier lives when we are smiling. Playfulness increases the frequency at which we smile. If we are boring and non-playful, it's almost as if life itself is saying, "If you're so bored, why do you need to be here?"

By Jenée Dana

All sorts of things can happen that are not in our best interest when we are in that frame of mind. But if we convince ourselves that there is much reason to be here, and that being here on the earth is a good thing, a happy thing, a fun thing, and that life is a good time, then we will continue to behave in ways that support that belief. What do you know? We actually become happier. Happiness is not a condition, it is a choice. Happy people do things that align themselves with the vibration of happiness.

The primary difference between having a "dream come true life" or not is listening to those ideas (the voice of the divine choreography of your life) and acting on them. When we listen to that voice, it will tell us to do things that follow a non-linear path. And therein lies the miraculous. Traditional paths lead to traditional results. If you want a non-traditional life, a magnificent life, then I have a newsflash for you: You are going to have to walk a magnificent path. While it could seem absurd on one level, putting syrup in my shoes was an opportunity for me to rehearse listening to the ideas as a way of life.

Now, this is no way to disrespect food. If you feel that this is wasteful, you can put the food in a plastic baggy and eat it later. If that doesn't sound appetizing, you can put little green soldiers in your socks. It's nothing more than a humorous secret between me and me so that I can smile instead of feeling nervous. I know it sounds nuts, but it really works.

Glenn Morshower

Don't Think Your DIBS Have to be "Hard"

Some people come from the school of thought that if your work is not "hard," it is not worth doing. They think that if you are not struggling constantly, anything you have achieved is not worth as much as something you had to bang your head against a wall for. Screw that! Yes, challenges do come up; HOWEVER, do not shy away from your strengths because you feel they come easy to you. Many of the millionaires in this world reached that level by doing what was easiest for them and charging a lot of money for it because it's not so easy for everyone else.

Call out your DIBS! Claim what is yours and go get it, without question. You can do anything you want to do in this world if you just believe that you can.

Chapter 6

Don't Get a Schedule Wedgie

Live By Your Values & Priorities
So You Can Have More Free Time

"It has been my observation that most people get ahead during the time that others waste."

Henry Ford

You would think that someone with ADHD would not be able to be very productive at all, right? While I do have a very short attention span, I have learned that I can still manage myself and get a lot done in a short amount of time with the right mindset and tools.

The main trick is really breaking things down into bite-size pieces so that when you look at what you need or want to do, you don't want to pull your hair out or punch someone in the face. These are not productive or constructive activities, and I don't recommend them.

Calendar Planner

After Chapter 5, you should have, or be intending to purchase, a calendar planner in order to help you achieve your goals and create more time. In your calendar, make sure you write down all the dates for the following:

- Class Schedule

- Study / Review notes after class

- Midterms

- Finals

- Work

- Special events

- Activities

- Exercise + Fun Activity = ACTIVIZE

- Meal Time

- Going out with friends / FUN

- Time with family

- Time to do nothing (rest!)

- Whatever else is fun for you

Anything important that needs to get done, or events you want to attend, need to go into your calendar. If it doesn't get scheduled, it most likely will not get done because you will forget about it.

Create a
My Values & Priorities Week

A My Values & Priorities Week (MVP Week) is an activity management tool that lets you plan your week so you can make sure you have time for all the things that are important to you, including time to go out with your friends.

If you don't like the idea of having to make a values and priority week, don't worry. I didn't either. I had a mentor assigned to me my freshman year in college. Erica told me that in order to get my work done and get good grades and have time for other things, I would need to make the weekly plan sheet. I thought she was a nut job because I already felt stressed and like I didn't have any time to spare. Now this crazy chick was asking me to take an extra 10-20 minutes to plan for things I already didn't have time for? Needless to say, I ignored her.

We met biweekly, and every time we met for the next four months and Erica asked if I had completed my weekly plan sheet, I told her, "I didn't have time." Again and again, she explained the importance of the weekly plan sheet and, again and again, I totally ignored her... until I finally got so sick of her asking me that I completed a weekly plan sheet just to shut her up.

Now, I really did like Erica a lot. I just thought the idea of a weekly plan sheet was absolutely stupid. To my surprise, a couple weeks after completing a WPS, I noticed that I felt way less stressed, was getting more work done, had more free time, and didn't know why.

Then I realized the only thing I had changed over the past couple weeks was making that stupid weekly plan sheet. I'm so happy that she was pleasantly persistent in bugging me to do a WPS. As I've used this over the years for myself and with my clients, I've realized that this is really an exercise in managing my values and priorities. So, I've changed the name to My Values & Priorities Week. Weekly plan sheet sounds too regimented to me.

Specific Instructions for Your MVP Week

Go to www.myfocusbook.com and enter your e-mail to sign up for the free online My Focus Book subscription. Check the Have Fun & Get It Done newsletter box so that I can send you your free weekly plan sheet with instructions. You can increase time with family and friends, check off a bucket list item or two, while achieving your definition of success.

Enter everything that you need to do and everything that is important to you into your MVP. Refer to the list of bulleted items at the beginning of the chapter to see what you are going to put in your sheet. Also, check out the small example of what a Values &

By Jenée Dana

Priorities Week looks like. You are going to want to color code your MVP so that you can quickly see at a glance what your week looks like. For example, if you color code orange for studying and blue for fun time and your week is full of orange and no blue (like Monica's was), you are going to have a visual to see what is unbalanced in your life. Then you can more easily make corrections because you are more aware of the problem.

Notice in the list in the beginning of the chapter, FUN is included in your MVP. You need to schedule your "me time" in order for it to really have a priority. Yes, FUN is a priority and when you make it a priority, you seem to get the "need-to's" done faster in order to have more time for your fun priorities.

Do you have anything fun planned this week?

If yes, what is it?

If no, what one thing would you like to do this week that would be awesome?

MVP — Study Time Tip

Reviewing your notes after class helps you retain the information better. I don't know the science behind it, or why it works, but it does. I didn't start doing this until my third year at UCLA, and I noticed that studying for my midterms and finals was much easier because I remembered more of the information. Make sure you schedule time for this in your MVP. It takes an hour or less only on the days that you have class, and it will likely end up being most of your study time, depending on your major.

MVP — Exercise Time Tip

When scheduling your exercise, I highly encourage you to find an exercise activity that you love doing. In fact, since the word exercise can sound pretty daunting at times, I came up with the word *activize,* because I choose activities that I love to do and that just happen to burn a lot of calories.

Some of my *activize* activities include Zumba (Latin dance aerobic), Hot Hula (Polynesian dance and muscle isolation), Cycling Class, Belly Dancing, Hiking, and Surfing. Running on the treadmill or elliptical for an hour does not cut it for me. It is so boring running on a machine in a gym watching CNN on the TV above you. Why do they put the news on, which is usually very depressing, to motivate people to run at the gym? I never understood that. Some people find running to be therapeutic, but I get distracted by squirrels and shiny things and need to be kept busy in my workout. That's just me. You figure out what works for you! And hey, if CNN motivates you to run in the gym, that's okay. No one is judging you.

By Jenée Dana

DIBS this week		Monday	Tuesday	Wednesday	Thursday	Friday	Saturday	Sunday
	8am	Breakfast	Breakfast	Breakfast	Breakfast	Breakfast	SLEEP IN	SLEEP IN
Spirituality	9am	Psych 101	Dance class	Psych 101	Dance class	p/t JOB	→	→
	10am	→	FREE	→	FREE	→	Breakfast	Breakfast
Health/"Me"	11am	Lunch	Lunch	Lunch	Lunch	→	BEACH	Family
	12pm	Comm 103	Geog 111	Comm 103	Geog 111	→	→	→
Family	1pm	→	→	→	→	Lunch	Lunch	Lunch
	2pm	Study/ Notes	Edu 80	Study/ Notes	Edu 80	FREE	BEACH	REST
Relationships	3pm	p/t JOB	→	p/t JOB	→	Get ready	→	REST
	4pm	→	Study/ Notes	→	Study/ Notes	For PARTY	FREE	REST
School/Career	5pm	Dinner	Dinner	Dinner	Dinner	Dinner		
	6pm		Dinner		Dinner		Dinner	Dinner
Giving Back	7pm		FREE TIME		FREE TIME			
	8pm							
FUN	9pm							

Daily List

Either in the daily or weekly sheet on your calendar (*My Focus Book* – hint! hint!), or on the day of your weekly section, make a list of all the things you need to do that day. Your Do It Bold Steps to get what you want come first on your list. Your errands and other activities are done after your Do It Bold Steps are completed. Pay attention to your body clock and schedule your work and study time when you work the best. If you are not a morning person, don't sweat it and don't schedule studying in the morning. Remember to include your fun time and time for meals.

> I lost all track of time while I was working on projects in college. Some days, I'd look up from a paper eight hours after I'd started writing and realize I hadn't eaten. The result? Thirty pounds attached themselves to me. My body thought I was trying to starve it to death, and it's taken years to get my metabolism back to normal. I still get lost in "the work zone", but now I know to make my phone beep at me at mealtimes.
>
> Amanda Johnson

Week of _____

I call DIBS Week Focus	Done In Bold Steps

- Finish studying by
  Thursday
	- Read notes after
	  class
	- Only read impt.
	  Concepts in Ch.

Complete by: 9.25.12	

Monday

9am Psych	☐	Read Ch.1 Psych
12pm Comm	☐	Syllabus in calendar
2pm 3pm Study	☐	Read Notes Psych
3pm 5pm Work	☐	Read Notes Comm
	☐	

Tuesday

9am Dance class	☐	Read Ch.1 Geog
12pm Geog	☐	Read Notes Geog
2pm Edu	☐	Read Notes Edu
4pm–5pm Study	☐	Dance my butt off
	☐	

Wednesday

9am Psych	☐	Read Ch.1 Comm
12pm Comm	☐	Read notes Psych
2pm –3pm Study	☐	Read notes Comm
3pm–5pm Work	☐	
	☐	

Notes:

Thursday
9am Dance class ☐ Read Ch.1 Geog
12pm Geog ☐ Read Notes Geog
2pm Edu ☐ Read Notes Edu
4pm-5pm Study ☐ Dance my butt off
☐

Friday
9am – 1pm p/t Job ☐ Get ready 4 PARTY
3pm Doctors ☐
9pm PARTY ☐
☐
☐

Saturday
11am – 4pm BEACH ☐ Go surfing
☐ Hang out with Adam
☐ Dinner with Katie
☐
☐

Sunday
10am Spiritual time ☐ Shopping with sis
11am – ☺ Hang out ☐ REST
with sis ☐
☐
☐

By Jenée Dana

MVP — Break Time Tip

Take breaks when studying or doing work. Depending on your attention span, you may want to take a five minute break every 30 minutes or a 10-15 minute break every hour. You are at full productivity when you're *in the zone*; however when you start to *zone out*, you need a break so you can clear your mind, get refreshed, and get back to work.

MVP — Work Time Tip

Yes, get a job or internship. Make sure that it seems like something fun to do. Not only are you going to manage your time better, you're going to make a little extra cash on the side, meet new people, and possibly make new friends.

In my freshman year, my mom did not want me to work. She worked full-time while going to school full-time and did not want me to have the same pressure or stress that she did. While I appreciated her concern and care for me, when I finally got a part-time job, I noticed that I was still able to get everything else done, AND I was making money, meeting new people, and valuing my time better because I had less time to fart around.

If you get an internship, you will be gaining valuable work experience in the field that you want to go into; or you may find out that the field you want to go into sucks and you can't see yourself doing this job for 30 years let alone two weeks. It's a great way to avoid spending all your time and energy on something only to realize AFTER you have the degree that you're going to hate the job. It's easy to change your major, but it's impossible to change the degree once you have it. With that said, I majored in Geography and

Environmental Studies and now I own a business and I am an author. It's okay to get a degree and go in a completely opposite direction too.

MVP — Take Care of Your Body Tip

After gaining about 20 pounds my senior year of high school, I was really worried about the infamous "Freshman 15". In case you haven't heard, the "Freshman 15" is where you gain 15 pounds your freshman year of college. That first month there, I ended up losing the 20 pounds that I had gained. Yes, I think I lost it a little too fast, BUT this is how I did it:

1. I was homesick, and it was a hot summer so the only food that appealed to me was soup and salad. I LOVE hot dogs, and even hot dogs grossed me out that first month. And it wasn't just because it was dorm food. UCLA's dorm food is actually pretty delicious.

2. Getting to class and back to my dorm was a workout. There were so many hills and stairs that my side was hurting after walking briskly to class. After climbing three massive hills to get back to my dorm, I had to climb another 80 steps (I counted) before I got to the entrance, then I had to take the stairs up to the second floor because I would get dirty looks from people in the elevator if I pressed the '2' button (because they were slow). Walk to class, even if there is a shuttle available. If your campus is spread out, consider riding a bike and you will avoid the evil poundage.

3. After losing the weight, I would usually eat an omelet with vegetables and no butter in the morning. I would have a salad with every meal with whatever healthy home-style options they

By Jenée Dana

were offering. And every Friday, I would have a hot dog (did I mention I love hot dogs?) and/or a burger with fries. And of course, during midterms and finals week, my roommate and I would treat ourselves to pizza with wings and ranch dressing as midnight snacks.

I kept off the weight, and that was all I did.

What commitment are you making for your health this week?

Exercise/Activize?

Food?

Can you walk to school/class?

Can you ride a bike to school/class?

15 Minutes Will Change Your Life

The planning aspect should not take a lot of time. Spend no more than 15 minutes on your values and priorities week. While I was in college, I would make an "ideal" values and priorities week for the quarter (one sheet for 3 months) so I had a routine. Routines are not bad as long as you have a FUN one. And there is always room for flexibility in your schedule when you truly know what your priorities are.

Value and Priority tools (most of them anyways) are not designed to give you more work and punish you. They are meant to put you in control of your schedule and your life so you can have time for FUN. I say that word a lot in this book and it never gets old. Don't be a robot that is just busy with busy work. Create a life that you want to live every day.

Chapter 7

"A Guerilla Ate Bacon Flavored Underwear" Got Me an A on My Midterm

Study "Less" and Learn More

"I never learn anything talking.
I only learn things when I ask questions."

Lou Holtz

The Brain Remembers FUN

One night I was pulling an all-nighter for a midterm in my communications class with Angie, Suzette and Chris. We were all worried about our grade because this class had a reputation for being very hard, and there was so much information to cover for the exam. Even though it was only an intro class, the Communications major was heavily impacted and they used this class to weed students out of the major. We were in a class of 400 students, all competing for a small number of As on the curve. We had to memorize initialisms (a group of letters used an abbreviation for an expression or name, with each letter pronounced separately) and explain them for the midterm. Initialisms are hard to remember because they don't sound like a word like acronyms do.

It was probably about three in the morning, and we were getting a little loopy. For one of the initialisms, we came up with the Guerrilla Ate Bacon Flavored Underwear for the test. I have no idea what that initialsm stands for today, but it proved to be very useful the next morning. We sat next to each other during the midterm, and when that question came up, we all started giggling under our breath. All of us did very well on the midterm, and I got an A. Sometimes you have to let loose and be silly because it is the funniest things that are the easiest to remember.

#1 — Study in Groups

Studying in groups is really effective and saves a lot of time.

• Study with people who don't already know everything

> It's not about studying with people who are smarter/not smarter than you. It is about selecting study buddies who don't already know it all. People who don't know everything are forced to seek out the answers, and the process of finding the answers generally yields better results (aka, remembering the concepts) than if you were to just ask Mr./Ms. Smartypants for the answers.
>
> Angie Tam

• Find people who have strengths in your weakest areas and vice versa

I am an awful note taker, but I (try to) listen in class. My friend Erin takes copious notes, but she just writes and doesn't pay attention to what is being taught (not sure how she does that, but whatever...). We ALWAYS tried to take our classes together! It helped that we were in the same major. As you can imagine, our arrangement worked out pretty well.

Angie Tam

> You don't remember much of what someone else teaches you, but you'll remember everything if you have to learn it well enough to teach others.
>
> Amanda Johnson

Teach each other

Have fun and be silly

You can get a good laugh coming up with initialisms like the Guerrilla Ate Bacon Flavored Underwear. Read a book on the beach. If you like the café vibe, study at Coffee Bean or Starbucks. Or take your laptop and sit on a lawn chair out by the pool. (Just don't drop it in the pool and be sure to wear plenty of sunscreen).

The more friends you make within your major, the easier it is to find study partners. You can also plan to take classes together like Angie did with Erin and I did with Angie.

Make friends in your classes

#2 — Take Good Notes or Find Someone Who Does

Mrs. Bayha, my world history teacher in high school, taught our class how to take really good notes. One of the main tools I learned from her is the use of abbreviations and symbols for common words and words used often for that particular class.

Here are just a few examples of note abbreviations that I use.

Use abbreviations →

Abbreviation	
Symbol	**Word**
IMPT	important
gov't	government
diff	different
Sep	separate
@	at
→	becomes
↑	increase
↓	decrease
<	less than
☹	I'm bored

By Jenée Dana

There is a good article at www.how-to-study.com that explains how to abbreviate words so they are still recognizable called 'Using Abbreviations to Write Notes Quickly'.

Use different colored pens and highlighters

Buy the multicolor pen package and take all the colors with you to class. Changing the pen color not only can make your notes look neater, it often helped me stay awake during really boring classes.

THIS IS IMPORTANT!!!

Whenever a professor says, "This is important", put a huge star next to it, or circle it, or write "IMPT!!!!" for *important* next to it. Sometimes the professor will just flat out say, "This is going to be on the test." Either way, they both mean the same thing–*Remember it!*

#3 – 80% Night before Midterm or Final

Angie, who consistently got great grades at UCLA, taught me that the night before a midterm or final, I only had to study 80% of the material. Within that 80%, I had to study 100% of all the items in my notes that had a huge star, or were circled, or had "IMPT!!!!" written next to it because I knew for sure that these would most likely be on the test. Be smart about how you study.

If the professor didn't spend a whole lot of time on it and didn't emphasize its importance, you don't need to spend your time on it either. If you use this study skill, you should get an A on the test. However, if during the test, you happen to forget a couple of important things from the 100% pile, and a couple of questions got asked from the 20% pile, worst-case scenario you probably get a B. Not too shabby.

#4 — Trade Notes

When you make new friends in your class, trade notes with them. It is pretty natural for me, even in an interesting class, to zone out for any length of time, come back to a state of awareness, and not know what the hell the professor is talking about. Imagine what that is like in a class that is complete crap-ola.

Some classes put the UCK in suck. I had an art history class held in an auditorium at 9am in comfy seats, and the professor would turn off the lights so we could see the images on the projector better. Had she not had the most monotone voice in the world, I might have actually stayed awake for that class. I learned art history in high school and enjoyed it. It wasn't fair, the seats were so comfortable. I tried hard not to fall asleep but it was inevitable. Therefore, I missed a whole lot of important material.

Thank God for my friend Deborah. For some reason, Deborah was immune to our professor's evil scheme to bore us to death and she would always let me look at her notes. Be smart about this though. Choose people who are serious about getting good grades or who are really interested in the subject. This isn't Slacker 101. I'm just saying, some GEs are unbearable, and you don't know it until it is too late.

Multiple Choice Tests

Multiple choice tests can seem easier; however they require us to remember more detail and a much broader scope of information than most essay type tests. And if you are like me, all of the possible options all over the test overloads my brain and makes me dizzy. One of my favorite professor's at UCLA, Professor Michael J. Vendrasco, gave me some very helpful tips for taking these tests. They don't always work 100% of the time, but you have a better shot if you are not 100% sure about the answer.

- The longest response is most often the correct one because the professor writing the test is more concerned with a well thought out answer. They won't spend a lot of time on something that is wrong.

- B and C are the most common answers. So if you are guessing blindly on a few questions, go with one or the other.

- If you see an answer you most definitely know is wrong, physically cross it out. This helps your brain to focus and visually narrow down your choices.

- If you see an answer you think might be correct, immediately circle it, and then check to see if another answer is better. Again this helps the brain to focus.

If you want more multiple choice tips, I found a good resource actually written by a professor. You can find it in the resources section. As you know, Google is an amazing thing. We have so much information at our finger tips. You can always Google "multiple choice study tips" to find even more information.

Essay Tips

Amanda Johnson, a book coach and owner of True to Intention (www.truetointention.com), wrote a lot of essays in college. She loves writing and is very good at it. She figured out a great way to save time when writing her papers.

In college, I learned to spend 90% of the project time developing a great outline and only 10% of the time filling in the blanks (or writing the paper).

Amanda Johnson

From my personal experience only, "DO NOT, I repeat DO NOT let the TA (teacher's assistant) read your essay to 'help' you with it before it is due."

Reason #1: They give crappy feedback.

During my freshman year, I wanted to be on top of things, so when the TAs encouraged us to turn our work in early so they could make multiple revisions of our essays I jumped at the offer thinking, "Wow, these wonderful people really want to help me." EHHHH WRONG! Every time I gave my paper to a TA before it was due, and followed all of their suggestions, I would get a B- on my essay (which would always count for a large portion of my grade).

When I asked my TA how this was possible, she said, "Just because you follow my suggestions and corrections, doesn't mean it will be an A paper." Uh, I'm sorry. I thought the whole point of taking our essays to these nerds ahead of time was so they would give us feedback in order to help us improve our grade. *Why would you give me B- feedback?* Mind you, this nitwit is the one grading my paper, not the professor.

Finally, I got sick of that crap after having three different classes/TAs with the same twisted mindset. I figured writing a B-paper the night before it was due was much easier than spending the time to make appointments for three to five different revision sessions only to be pissed off in the end. Something MIRACULOUS happened. I started getting As on my essays and reports, with a B+ here and there. Why? Read on.

Reason #2: They seem to get sick of it.

If you give your paper to the TA before it is due, I believe they get sick of reading it by the time grading comes around. That is the only logical explanation I can come up with, besides the fact that my TA for my sociology class was possibly a lunatic.

My friend Katie got straight As as an English major at UCLA. Here are a few tips from her on how to write a good essay.

1. Know what your teacher is looking for!

- New to college? Take an introductory writing course to learn the specific expectations of your university. Trust me, even if you pass the AP exam with flying colors, you may not earn an A on your first college paper. Instructors are more forgiving with their grades in these courses because they understand that students are just learning. It's a safe place to assess your writing skills at the college level. Also, they usually teach you how to navigate the college's online database as well as the confusing library system.

2. T-S-A
 • Follow the paragraph format:
   Topic, Support, and Analysis. Each
   paragraph should begin with a clear
   statement of the topic followed by
   multiple pieces of support (examples)
   and analysis of how these examples
   prove your point.

3. You really do get an A for effort.
 • Putting effort into your papers is the
   best way to ensure a good grade.
   This means effort throughout the
   writing process. So take the time for
   prewriting, organization of ideas,
   revision, and proofreading. Sloppy
   mistakes are the easiest way
   to distinguish the dedicated students
   from the students who hastily
   complete their work. Put in the
   extra effort.

Katie Ramos

Reading Tips

Keep up with your reading...or not. Danny suggests you keep up with your readings. At the very least, readings supplement what the professor is talking about. Katie had to read everything the professor gave her because she was an English major and was usually writing essays on novels. Math majors usually have less reading involved, but they have more homework.

I, on the other hand, have always had trouble reading. I read very slowly, and recently, it was recommended that I get tested for dyslexia.

Needless to say, I always skipped reading if I felt the professor included the material as fluff. I would also read the questions in the back of the chapter and just skim for the answers. And I would use the texts to get more information when a specific concept the professor went over was still unclear to me.

By Jenée Dana

Prioritize

If you are good at one class, make sure to concentrate more on the class you are unsure about.

Figure out what works for you. Almost every freshman at UCLA has trouble their first few quarters as they try and develop their own study habits.

Danny Roddy

Take Advantage of Office Hours

If you are having trouble with a concept in class, go to the professor's office hours. Surprisingly, most students do not utilize this. I was usually the only one in office hours in a hard class, and rarely would someone else stop by. Most professors really appreciate the fact that you actually want to learn and they are happy to explain things to you.

Learning Disabilities Offices at Universities

Professor Gillespie told me about the Students with Learning Disabilities office at UCLA after I told him that I was having a hard time paying attention, even though I really liked his class. (I actually meant that.)

At first I was embarrassed to go the office and get tested, but then I realized that everyone has strengths and perceived weaknesses. I was just getting help so I could spend more time focusing on and utilizing my strengths.

Do What Feels Right

Take tips from here that resonate with you and make sense. When you're studying with other friends that get good grades, ask them what they do. There truly is no such thing as a stupid question.

Larry Broughton, an extremely successful business owner (who built Broughton Hospitality, a leader in the boutique hotel industry, to grossing $250 million dollars per year), attributes much of his accomplishment to not being afraid to ask "dumb" questions as well as to building teams where individuals complement each other's strengths.

These skills work in school, and they work in life.

Chapter 8

The Underwear Run

Managing Your Real Life Social Network

> "I never did a day's work in my life.
> It was all fun."
>
> *Thomas A. Edison*

The underwear run is a famous tradition at UCLA. One night every year, students allegedly strip down to their underwear and run together down Fraternity Row. When I say underwear, it is nothing grotesque...just mostly sports bras and boxer shorts. I never participated in this lovely tradition, but I know others that did and had a blast. The point is: Lots of colleges have fun little weird traditions and activities that bring students together in a fun way. College is a time to have fun and meet new people. Just be safe and don't do anything that will get you arrested.

Create Boundaries for Roommates

My first summer school session at UCLA was an eye-opening experience. I was living in a cramped room with two other girls. We all had to make roommate agreements with our Resident Assistant and sign them together. One of my roommates said, "Absolutely no sex in the dorm room, whether I am in the room or not." My other roommate and I glanced at each other, thinking, "Why would you care if no one is in the room?" but we signed the agreement because it didn't matter. It wasn't going to happen anyways.

A week and half later my allegedly "celibate" roommate allegedly brought three large guys up to our dorm room. It was already 10pm, and I had a 7am class so I was ready to go to sleep. One of the guys was so tall his head was above my top bunk bed. It seemed like my roommate was really close with these boys, so I just thought they were visiting from back home. They stayed and talked for awhile and then two of the boys left, while the other guy *allegedly* climbed into bed with my roommate. I was not alarmed because she was so adamant about NO SEX. I assumed it was her boyfriend from high school, they missed each other, and they were just going to snuggle before he left.

Well, she *allegedly* (I learned well from Kathy Griffin on how to tell a story without getting sued) BROKE her own rule. The next morning, I asked my other roommate, "Were you awake?"

"Yeah," she replied.

"What the hell?!?! Is this girl on crack?" I couldn't believe she'd made such a big stink about this and then broke the rule herself while we were in the room.

The kicker? She didn't even know those guys; she had met them three days earlier at a restaurant.

If we were going to be living with each other all year, I would have talked to the RA and had her kicked out of our room, but since we were only going to be living with each other for a couple more weeks,

I counted down the days until my next roommate would arrive, and only spoke with my other really nice roommate.

I am not trying to scare you. This doesn't happen to most people. Just be aware that you need to be clear with your roommates about what is acceptable and what is not. It is difficult, living with one new person, let along two in one room. So, with my next roommates I made sure to tell them what my boundaries were and warned them that if they ever did that to me, I would severely embarrass them.

What do you want
in a roommate?

What are you willing to tolerate,
and what is a deal-breaker?

How will you communicate that to
your roommate up front?

Find Your People

It is so important to make friends – the *right* friends. I remember when I first got to UCLA, there was some serious culture shock for me. I felt so out of place. And then I started to hang out with a crowd that was not like-minded. I started to notice I didn't like the people I was hanging around very much. Not that I didn't like them personally, I just didn't like how I felt during or after we hung out. We didn't have the same values and I just felt like I didn't fit in or belong. Some of my friends' family members also didn't accept me at first because of my race (yeah, we are in the 21st century). I felt left out and just wanted some commonality with someone. After realizing this, I changed my scene and felt much better and happier about the people I was choosing to be around.

How do you find your people?

- Join clubs
- Join sports

Grab coffee or lunch with someone from class

> I am in the fraternity Sigma Pi at UCLA. I have done BJJ (Brazilian Jiu-Jitsu), starting my sophomore year, and numerous IM sports. I have also done many other activities throughout my first 2 1/3 quarters such as Habitat for Humanity or Project Literacy. Like high school, I wanted to try a bunch of new things.
>
> Danny Roddy

By Jenée Dana

It's a good way to 'test someone out' in a public place. By doing this, you will figure out if this is someone you would like to hang around or at least cool enough to study with.

go to parties

Yes, I said go to parties. Just make sure that you act responsibly by having a designated driver, and that your major isn't partying unless you are an event planner. Try and schedule your classes to end on Thursday, get your studying done that day, and then you will have a 3 day weekend to go to a party, go to work, or go to the beach. The weekend is yours.

Manage Relationships with "Not Your People"

Self-made millionaire and successful author Jim Rohn says, "You are the average of the five people you spend the most time with."

Do you even like the people you are hanging out with? Do you admire them in any way? If not, BAIL! Run as fast as you can! They are not the right people to support you in your goals. You can still be nice to them; just keep them out of your backyard, figuratively and possibly literally. Have an imaginary fence where you can say, "Hi," and wave to these people from a safe distance. The fence will protect you from dealing with them on a regular basis.

Networking

Networking is a great thing to do in college. Your first priority, beyond getting the grades, should always be to make great friends, keeping your future in mind. Think about those in power and many of our leaders in this country. Did they get their positions because they were the absolute best at what they do? Not necessarily. Many of them built great relationships and connections throughout their life and never gave up on what they decided they wanted. Craig Duswalt, creator of the Rockstar System for Success, says, "It's not who you know, it's who knows you."

It's also a good idea to keep in touch with acquaintances or professors through Linkedin or Facebook. Meet up with those you click with every now and then.

By expanding your network, you expand the possibilities and opportunities for yourself in your future career. If there is a job opening or a great business opportunity, who do you think is going to get recommended? You, if you are friends with them and they know you are qualified and will deliver results. And vice versa. Remember that merit is still a key factor in this system. Being someone's friend just gives them an indication that you can be a part of the team and are easy to work with. You have to be able to pull your weight and deliver on the expectations set for you. Most importantly, you don't always want to be on the "taking" end of the stick. Helping friends out whenever you can is a part of life.

Have Fun!!!

This is the most important! Have fun! When you lose the fun in your life, you start to die inside. Have you seen people that are not having fun in life anymore? It's depressing just talking to them. Plan for those lazy days where you rest and take care of yourself so you can have the energy to work full blast after. Having fun doesn't mean dropping your responsibilities, but it does mean "drop the dime". By drop the dime, I mean that thing you're clenching between your booty-cheeks. Being an adult does not mean "Grow up, forget childish things, and be uptight." Who thought that crap up anyways? Define what fun means to you, and go make it happen.

They used to say high school years were the best of your life. Now they say college years are the best years of your life. I disagree. Yes, high school and college were fun, but do they have to be the best? So what those people are really saying is, "Just give up on having the best life possible after college. It is all downhill from there." Uggghh...that is so sad. They probably made some bad decisions and never took action to correct them. These are not the people you want to listen to. College is *the beginning* of the best years of your life. The rest of your life is what you make it to be. Don't let anyone tell you otherwise! It's your choice. Do you want a train wreck of a life, or a life to be excited about? You decide, and go get it. Period! ☺

Afterword

After You Put On Your Underwear, Don't Walk Out the Door Without Your Pants

"I believe that being successful means
having a balance of success stories across
the many areas of your life. You can't truly
be considered successful in your business
life if your home life is in shambles."

Zig Ziglar

You read the book. I hope you enjoyed it. Now what? Whether you want to graduate early or you just want to get a handle on your values and priorities so you can have even more time for fun, the most important step is the first.

You need a planner system that works for you. This is key in order to reduce stress and be in control of your life. If you don't control your schedule, someone else will. If you already have a planner system, awesome! If you are still looking for a system that is right for you and you like the *My Focus Book* style, you have two options:

#1—If you are an electronic planner type person, go to **www.myfocusbook.com** and sign up for the online *My Focus Book*. It is *free*, so what do you have to lose, right?

#2–If you are a paper planner type person and like to write things down, go to **www.myfocusbook.com** where you can check out and purchase a paper planner version of *My Focus Book*.

If you would like more information and tips on how to have fun and get it done, check out my blog and sign up for the free student newsletter at **www.myfocusbook.com.**

I am a firm believer that you can read all day long, but until you have applied what you have learned in real life, words can be easily forgotten.

Get started today. Whether it is with *My Focus Book* or another system, it doesn't matter as long as you start.

Hugs, Belief & Abundance,
Jenée Dana

P.S. Please keep in touch. I want to hear how you decide to use the tips and suggestions I shared in this book. Fill me in on your successes. Ask questions. Let me know how I can help.

Email: **Jenée@myfocusbook.com**
Office: **1-855-No-Wedgie**

By Jenée Dana

To use the *free* version of My Focus Book web app and get
free Have Fun & Get It Done tips emailed to you,
sign up at:
www.myfocusbook.com

To have Jenée speak at your school or event,
please contact:
speak@myfocusbook.com

To order books or planners in bulk for a discount, contact:
Jenée@myfocusbook.com

To purchase planners or books individually go to:
www.myfocusbook.com

By Jenée Dana

About the Author

Jenée Dana, Chief Focusing Officer of *My Focus Book* and author of *Have Fun & Get It Done: Graduate from a Top University in 3 Years or Less Without Being a Genius,* acquired much of her expertise in productivity while earning her Bachelor of Arts degree from UCLA. After two grueling years of struggling with undiagnosed reading disabilities and ADHD, Jenée took a risk to relieve her mother of the financial burden and decided to complete her last two years of UCLA academic requirements in just one year. Combining the best productivity tools she could get her hands on, she had her most productive and exciting year ever. Her grades went up, and so did her fun factor! Today, she teaches students, entrepreneurs, and professionals how to increase their productivity and reach their goals without sacrificing the fun.

Since graduating UCLA, she realized the importance and value of the productivity skills she had learned from books, friends, and good old trial and error. She created *My Focus Book* for herself originally to keep everything she needed to achieve her goals and stay on track in one place. Thanks to her ADHD, she loses things or misplaces them often, and *My Focus Book* was a way to keep her head on straight. A professional Mary Kay Senior Beauty Consultant at the time, her unit saw the new planner she was using and asked her to make them one. That year, two women in her adoptee unit earned their free Mary Kay cars and became Directors, attributing their success to the *My Focus Book.* Her entire unit encouraged her to start her business and *My Focus Book* was born.

Since then, she has been supporting clients all over the United States and Canada. *My Focus Book* has helped top executives in multi-million dollar personal development companies to reach their goals faster. She has had clients report up to 100% increase in their productivity using her Daily Accountability sheets.

Since writing *Have Fun & Get It Done: Graduate From a Top University in 3 Years or Less Without Being a Genius,* she has been asked to speak to organizations, businesses and schools about how they can increase their productivity and still have time for a life. Now a student version, as well as an online version, of the *My Focus Book* bucket list calendar has been created.

Jenée Dana resides in Hawaii with her fiancé Adam. She runs Have Fun & Get It Done Networking activities with Zumba instructors and speaks to organizations, schools, and businesses about productivity and the Have Fun & Get It Done system. When Jenée is not working, she is having fun on a date with Adam, having lunch with a friend, "activizing", or shopping.

By Jenée Dana

Notes

Chapter 1

Page "Living On Campus/Off Campus/With Parents...": California Post-Secondary Education Commission, 2009-2010, released February 15, 2011 at: www.cpec.ca.gov/completereports/2011 reports/11-01.pdf.

Page "Living On Campus/Off Campus/With Parents...": California State University, 2010-2011, at: www.calstate.edu/sas/documents/2010 -11COA.pdf.

Page "Living On Campus/Off Campus/With Parents...": University of California Berkeley, 2011-2012, at: http://students.berkeley.edu/finaid/ home/cost.htm.

Page "Living On Campus/Off Campus/With Parents...": University of California Davis, 2010-2011, at: http://facts.ucdavis.edu/undergraduate cost_of_attendance.lasso.

Page "Living On Campus/Off Campus/With Parents...": University of California Irvine, 2011-2012, at: http://www.ofas.uci.edu/content/costs .aspx?nav=1.

Page "Living On Campus/Off Campus/With Parents...": University of California Los Angeles, 2011-2012, at: http://www.fao.ucla.edu/ publications/2011-2012/Budgets%20for%20Web%20revised%20for%20tuition%20increase.pdf.

Page "Living On Campus/Off Campus/With Parents...": University of California Merced, 2009-2010, at: http://financialaid.ucmerced.edu/ current-students/cost-attendance.

Page "Living On Campus/Off Campus/With Parents...": University of California Riverside, 2011-2012, at: http://finaid.ucr.edu/UCRCost/ Pages/default.aspx.

Page "Living On Campus/Off Campus/With Parents...": University of California San Diego, 2011-2012, at: http://students.ucsd.edu/ finances/financial-aid/budgeting/undergrad-20112012.html.

Page "Living On Campus/Off Campus/With Parents...": University of California Santa Barbara, 2010-2011, at: http://parenthandbook. sa.ucsb.edu/campusissues/moneymatters.aspx.

Page "Living On Campus/Off Campus/With Parents...": University of California Santa Cruz, 2010-2011, at: http://financialaid.ucsc.edu/ ugradbudget1011.shtml.

Page "Living On Campus/Off Campus/With Parents...": University of Southern California, 2011-2012, at: http://www.usc.edu/admission/fa /applying_receiving/undergraduates2/costs.html

Page "Living On Campus/Off Campus/With Parents...": University of La Verne, 2011-2012, at: http://laverne.edu/tuition/undergraduate-traditional/

Page "Living On Campus/Off Campus/With Parents...": Chapman University, 2011-2012, at: http://www.chapman.edu/sbs/tuition/FeeInfo1.asp.

Page "Financial Aid & Grants...": Lew, Phillip. Phillip Lew's College Planning System for Success. Santa Clarita: College Planning Experts Inc, 2009, pp.66-70.

Page "Why Pay Retail for College?: Table, ibid.

Chapter 3

Page "For example: The Reticular Activating System...": Canfield, Jack. The Success Principles: How to Get From Where You Are To Where You Want To Be. New York: Collins, 2007, pp.81-83, 90.

Chapter 5

Page "Success on My Terms is an exercise...": My Focus Book, LLC, at: www.myfocusbook.com

Page "Everything I Want to Accomplish, Acquire, and Become, Before I Kick the Bucket ...": My Focus Book, LLC, at:www.myfocusbook.com

Page "My Focus Book Calendar ...": My Focus Book, LLC, at:www.myfocusbook.com

Chapter 6

Page "Weekly Plan Sheet...": My Focus Book, LLC, at: www.myfocusbook.com

Page "Weekly Calendar...": My Focus Book, LLC, at: www.myfocusbook.com

Chapter 7

Page "Multiple Choice Tests...": University of Wisconsin-Eau Claire, at: http://www.uwec.edu/ geography/ivogeler/multiple.htm

Resources

Chapter 2

For help with financial aid and college planning:

Phillip Lew and Trevor Ramos

www.totalcollegesolutions.com

For help with School Event Productions (Staging, Lighting, Video, Sound, DJ):

www.SOSentertainment.com

Chapter 3

For help with tutoring, essay writing, college admissions/planning or career planning:

Maka Marketing with Monica Shukla
www.advancetocollege.com

One Great Goal with Ursula Mentjes
www.salescoachnow.com

The Success Principles by Jack Canfield
www.thesuccessprinciples.com

For help writing a book:

Transformational Book Coach Amanda Johnson

www.truetointention.com

For help with creatively living on a college-budget and wealth management:

The Smart Cookies

www.smartcookies.com

Chapter 4

For help with getting information on a professor before you sign up for their class...

www.ratemyprofessors.com

Chapter 5

For more info on how to attend Glenn Morshower's The Extra Mile seminar

www.GlennMorshower.com

Chapter 6

For more information on how to *activize* with Zumba:

www.zumba.com

For more information on how to *activize* with Hot Hula Fitness

www.anna-rita.com

Check out your Universities gym on campus and see what activities / classes they have that sound fun to you.

Chapter 7

Learn how to abbreviate words

www.how-to-study.com

Learn how to take multiple choice tests

http://www.uwec.edu/geography/ivogeler/multiple.htm